The General
Trading Company

Other Titles of Interest from Lexington Books:

Entry Strategies for International Markets
Franklin R. Root, The Wharton School,
University of Pennsylvania
ISBN 0-669-13701-4   288 pages $29.00

The Trade and Tariff Act of 1984
Trade Policy in the Reagan Administration
Stephen L. Lande, Manchester Associates, Ltd., and
Craig VanGrasstek, Korean Traders Association
ISBN 0-669-12007-3   176 pages $21.00

Multinational Corporate Strategy
Planning for World Markets
James C. Leontiades
Foreword by H. Igor Ansoff
ISBN 0-669-07381-4   256 pages $28.00

Multinational Corporations
The Political Economy of Foreign Direct Investment
Theodore H. Moran, Georgetown School of Foreign
Service, editor
ISBN 0-669-11241-0   304 pages $29.00

Strategies for Joint Ventures
Kathryn Rudie Harrigan, Columbia University
Foreword by William H. Newman
ISBN 0-669-10448-5   448 pages $32.00

From Patron to Partner
*The Development of U.S.–Korean Business and
Trade Relations*
Karl Moskowitz, Harvard University, editor
ISBN 0-669-06837-3   256 pages $28.00

The General Trading Company

Concept and Strategy

Dong-Sung Cho
Seoul National University

Lexington Books
D.C. Heath and Company/Lexington, Massachusetts/Toronto

Library of Congress Cataloging-in-Publication Data
Cho, Dong-Sung.
   The general trading company.

   Bibliography: p.
   Includes index.
   1. Trading companies. I. Title.
HF1009.5.C52   1987   382   86-45755
ISBN 0-669-14296-4

Published simultaneously in Canada
Printed in the United States of America
Casebound International Standard Book Number: 0-669-14296-4
Library of Congress Catalog Card Number: 86-45755

The paper used in this publication meets the minimum requirements of
American National Standard for Information Sciences—Permanence of
Paper for Printed Library Materials, ANSI Z39.48-1984.
∞ ™

87 88 89 90 8 7 6 5 4 3 2 1

To Dae-hwan, Jeong-hwan, Stephanie, and Insook

Contents

Figures

Tables

Foreword

Robert Stobaugh

I was particularly pleased to read this book. My research interests in the international business field have focused on the activities of multinational enterprises, that is, large companies that manufacture in a number of countries. I knew little about trading companies, so this provided an opportunity to learn. I was not disappointed.

The subject obviously is of great importance. Even the casual observer knows of the essential role of the Japanese trading companies in aiding Japanese exports. And observers familar with international business know of the importance of Korean trading companies and of the attempt by the U.S. government to encourage U.S. export trading companies.

Previous studies of trading companies have tended to focus on Japanese trading companies—the *sogo-shosha*. Professor Cho uses these studies as well as his own research to conclude that the Japanese trading companies, although more fully developed than trading companies headquartered elsewhere, face an uncertain future. This is a very important conclusion given the significant role played by the *sogo-shosha* in Japan's industrial development.

The author also studied trading companies headquartered in Europe, Korea, Taiwan, Thailand, Turkey, and the United States. He is the first researcher to study such firms in so many countries. He uses these results to develop a model applicable to all trading companies. In so doing, he puts to rest the notion expounded by some authors that trading companies are but one step in the development of a multinational enterprise.

His model is a readily usable, easily remembered way of viewing trading companies. Not only is the model of great interest but so is the discussion of the eight generic strategies that he draws from the model.

The book obviously breaks important, new ground. It also has the advantage of being written in clear English without the economic and business jargon that often mars academic studies. I strongly recommend the book to business executives, academics, and government officials.

Preface and Acknowledgments

During the 1870s, the Japanese government established national trading companies to gain economic independence from foreign traders. In the 1890s, it used these companies to internationalize domestic industries. Japanese trading companies consolidated the trading activities and facilitated the exports of domestic manufacturers, who at that time lacked the ability independently to penetrate overseas markets. Thus *sogo-shosha*, or Japanese general trading companies (GTCs), evolved.

In contrast, manufacturing companies in the United States internationalized their operations mainly through their own efforts, after establishing themselves in the domestic market. Instead of relying on trading companies, they chose direct investment as a mode of foreign involvement, emerging as multinational corporations (MNCs).

Scholars have applied their theories of the multinational corporation to explain the *sogo-shosha*, for example, viewing *sogo-shosha* as an incomplete or transformed, Japan-style MNC. Such viewpoints evaluate *sogo-shosha* against existing analyses of the MNC and tacitly assume that the MNC is the only means of internationalizing domestic industries. Such viewpoints do not consider the GTC as a viable alternative to the MNC in the internationalization of domestic businesses.

However, the GTC is no longer unique to Japan. Many other countries, including Korea, Taiwan, Thailand, and Turkey, have adopted the GTC or similar organizational forms for promoting the internationalization of their economy. With the passage of the Export Trading Company Act of 1982, even the United States has now its own version of the GTC, with goals and purposes similar to those previously formed in other countries.

Given this increasing acceptance of the GTC as a viable form of international business organization, it is time to examine critically the GTC with a conceptual framework unbounded by theories of the MNC. The purpose of this book, therefore, is to derive a concept of the GTC as a general form of business entity, rather than as a particular case witnessed in a few places such as Japan and Korea.

Chapter 1 reviews the historical evolution of the GTC over the past four centuries. Chapter 2 defines the concept of the GTC through a quantitative approach. It compares four international business forms—Japanese GTCs, Korean GTCs, U.S.-based MNCs, and European trading houses—to reach a concept of the GTC that emphasizes the synergy effect arising from area, product, and functional diversification. Chapter 3 compares the Japanese GTC and the U.S.-MNC, describing the differences in their business strategies.

Chapter 4 describes the establishment and growth of GTCs in Japan, Korea, Taiwan, Thailand, Turkey, and the United States. It provides an understanding of the diversity among various GTCs, substantiating the proposition that the GTC is not a monolith but a variable concept conducive to local adaptation. Chapter 5 describes the alternative strategies that a trading company can choose. Although chapter 2 indicates that the optimal strategy for a GTC is to pursue full product, area, and functional diversification, there are in fact seven other strategic options available to any trading company. Each of these alternatives is identified and analyzed.

This book results from my seven years of research into the topic, beginning in 1978 when I returned to Seoul National University after several years of studying, teaching and working in American business schools and in a multinational coporation. The first course I was to teach in Korea was international business. Theories and practices of foreign direct investment and multinational corporations, primarily based on Western experiences, could not meet the needs of the Korean students, who were eager to learn how they could internationalize Korean business activities. Frustrated, I searched and spotted several Korean GTCs, which were rapidly transforming the Korean economy into an internationally viable force through aggressive marketing efforts abroad. I decided to study those firms for myself and to transmit the research result to my students. The behavorial and strategic patterns of these GTCs could not be easily explained by literature existing at that time. As a result, I plunged into this research, which was a virgin territory to business scholars.

I received support in various forms. The Ministry of Commerce and Industry of the Korean Government first requested me to explore the problems that Korean GTCs faced in the wake of the deteriorating world economy in the late 1970s. This project enabled me to make an extensive study of the GTC by interviewing approximately 300 policymakers, practitioners, and academicians in Korea, Japan, the United States, Europe, and other countries. Among those I interviewed, I am most grateful to Messrs. Ryuzo Sejima, former chairman of C. Itoh & Co., and Chong-Hyun Chey, chairman of Sunkyong group. The study also required the analysis of several million pieces of statistical data compiled by the GTCs and my staff of five research associates (Dong-Kee Lee, currently a doctoral candidate at New York University; Sung-Tai Hong, a doctoral candidate at University of Illinois; Jeong-Myung Kim, a doctoral candidate at the Ohio State University; Dong-Hyun Ji, a doctoral candidate at the

Wharton School; and Young-Do Kim). The study was completed in the summer of 1981.

My second round of research was a historic review of trading companies from the mercantilistic era to the present and a comparison of present-day GTCs in different countries. This study laid a foundation on which to generate a conceptual definition of the GTC. The result of this study was published as a two-volume book in Korea in 1983.

In the 1983–84 academic year, I spent my sabbatical year in the United States as a visiting associate professor at the Harvard Business School, where I presented my research findings at the doctoral seminar and various other occasions. Professors Robert Stobaugh, Francis Aguilar, and James Heskett warmly encouraged me to publish my research findings in English. Ms. Caroline McCarley of Lexington Books kindly offered to publish my text. Jeong-Ho Song, Sung-Joo Lee, Joo-heon Kim, Gun-sang Son, and Dong-Jae Kim helped me prepare the manuscript in English, while Ms. Barbara Feinberg and Ms. Nancy Herndon lent their expert editorial skills to improve the style and format. Professor Henri-Claude de Bettignies also helped me conduct additional research on European trading companies by inviting me as a visiting professor to INSEAD in 1985. Professors Sang-Kee Min and Yoo-Keun Shin as well as Deans Yong-Joon Lee and Byung-Koo Shim of Seoul National University helped me conduct research without being interrupted by administrative problems. Throughout these chaotic years, my three children, Dae-hwan, Jeong-hwan, and Stephanie, supplied me with ample sources of relaxation, while my wife Insook supported me with unfailing trust in my ability to complete the task. In spite of all this support and ecouragement, I take full responsibility for any mistakes or errors that might be present in this book.

1
Trading Companies: A Historical Perspective

G eneral trading companies are a relatively new phenomenon in the international business scene. In the late 1950s, after the regrouping of Mitsubishi and Mitsui, Japanese newspapers started to describe a group of large Japanese trading companies as *sogo-shosha*. We have since come to understand *sogo-shosha*, loosely translated as *general trading company* (GTC), as a generic term for large trading companies in Japan.

During the 1970s, governments of newly industrializing countries such as Korea, Taiwan, Thailand, and Turkey began to develop their own GTC systems to promote exportation in the face of increasing trade protectionism among the major importing countries. In 1982, even the United States, a nation with an advanced economy, established its own version of the GTC to promote its export activities. With this evolution of the GTC as an influential actor in the international business scene, a growing interest has developed among practitioners and academicians in the nature and behavior of the GTC. Research in this area, however, is such that even a basic concept, let alone a general theory, remains to be clearly defined.

This chapter examines the birth and growth of the GTC to give a systematic understanding of the GTC as an international business entity. The history of the GTC can be divided into three stages: its origin from European trading houses in the seventeenth century; its development by Japanese trading companies in the nineteenth and twentieth centuries; and its spread to other countries such as Korea, Taiwan, and the United States since the mid-1970s. The historic analysis provides a basis on which a general theory of the GTC may be developed.

The Origin of the GTC: European Trading Houses

The opening of the sea route from Europe to India via the Cape of Good Hope by Vasco de Gama in 1498 created new trade opportunities for European merchants. The initial trading activities were conducted by Portuguese, Spanish, Dutch, British, and French adventurers, backed by merchant capitals through joint partnerships such as the Company of Merchant Adventurers of England.[1] Soon the monarchs of Europe, hoping to expand their imperial powers and wealth, chartered the traders to form corporate bodies that enjoyed exclusive proprietorship in specific areas and protection by the naval forces in exchange for export taxes. As a result, the East India Company of the Netherlands (*Oost-Indische Compagnie*) was formed in 1602, followed shortly by the British East India Company and the French East India Company (*La Compagnie des Indes*).

These pioneering companies began their trading activities in India and nearby territories. Each was furnished with royal charters by its home country, which gave it not only the exclusive right to engage in trade, but also a blanket endorsement for making war, concluding treaties, acquiring territories and building fortresses to protect its territorial right.[2] Indeed, the distinguishing feature of these companies was their possession of monopoly control over the region where they conducted their trading activities. According to the renowned historian James Mill:

> During that age, the principles of public wealth were very imperfectly understood and hardly any trade was regarded as profitable but that which was exclusive. The different nations which traded to India, all traded by way of monopoly; and the several exclusive companies treated every proposal for a participation in their traffic, as a proposal for their ruin. In the same spirit, every nation which obtained admittance into any newly explored channel of commerce endeavored to exclude from it all participators, and considered its own profits as depending on the absence of all competition.[3]

Naturally, these trading companies built their business around the colonies over which their home governments claimed imperial suzerainty. The British emerged as the monopolistic proprietor of India, while the Dutch took control of Sumatra, Java, and other nearby archipelagos which were then known as the Spice Islands and later became the Netherlands East Indies.[4] French merchants went further to the east and anchored in the Mekong delta, later extending their rule over Cochin China, Cambodia, and Laos, and eventually controlling the peninsula of Indo-China.[5] The Spanish went further to the east, reaching the Philippines and establishing a colonial base there. Within the colonies, they diversified from trading of basic materials like indigo, pepper, sugar, tea, saltpeter, metals, and silk[6] to a more systematic extraction of the resources of the region through estate-farming, mining and extraction, and usury.[7]

After establishing a strong foothold on the colonial territories of South and Southeast Asia, European traders moved eastward and eventually reached Japan. The East India Company of the Netherlands and British East India

Company set up trading posts at Hirado, an island off the northwest coast of Kyushu, in 1609 and 1613, respectively. The English post was closed down eleven years later, while the Dutch one was moved to a small island in Nagasaki harbor.[8] The Dutch company held a virtual monopoly of foreign trade in Japan and cultivated its connection with the Tokugawa Shogunate, the Japanese rulers in the seventeenth century. The Shogunate, however, adopted a policy of closing the country to foreign trade, confining the activities of the Dutch traders to the Nagasaki area.[9]

In 1853, Commodore Mathew Perry of the U.S. Navy forced the Shogunate to abandon its isolationist policy. The European empires quickly followed the United States into Japan and set up business concerns in Yokohama near Edo (now Tokyo) and in Hyogo (now Kobe) near Osaka. These events disclosed the weakness of the Shogunate military power and provided a cause for young samurai from Satsuma and Choshu provinces to rally under the slogan of "expel the barbarians."[10] This movement culminated in the Meiji Restoration, which, in 1868, ended the Shogunate government and restored the imperial rule by Matsuhito.[11]

In the meantime, however, European trading companies had dominated Japan's import market, controlling 95.3 percent of imports in 1876. This dominance was mainly attributed to the Europeans' superior vessels and long trading experience, but a more important reason lay in the unfair treaties that European empires had forced Japan to accept. For example, the Shogunate in 1866 accepted a tariff rate fixed as low as 5 percent, which opened the country to a flood of Western manufactured goods, undermining many traditional industries. According to Edwin O. Reischauer, an authority on Japan, "There was a desperate need to industrialize the country if Japan were to protect herself from Western economic domination and build the sort of economy that could support a military establishment that would provide security from the West."[12]

In order to reduce the chronic dependence of Japan on the European traders for much needed imports, the Meiji government promoted the establishment of national trading companies. Government assistance and protection were offered to willing merchants. The House of Mitsui, known for over a century as an influential apparel dealer and banker, complied with the government's offer, establishing in 1876 Mitsui Bussan to engage in direct foreign trade. In 1870 Iwasaki Yataro established a shipping company called Tsukumo Shokai in Osaka, renamed Mitsubishi Trading Company in 1873. Other commercial houses included C. Itoh (later split to C. Itoh and Marubeni), established in 1872, and Suzuki Shoten (which later became Nissho), established in 1877.[13] These trading companies, which initially focused on import markets, have since developed into huge trading organizations with globally integrated activities. They are today's *sogo-shosha*.

Development of the GTC: Japanese *Sogo-Shosha*

Originally, the Japanese trading companies were not a uniquely Japanese form of business organization. The Meiji government established trading companies by modeling them after the European trading houses. Like European trading houses, Japanese trading companies were conceived to conduct trade, rather than growing out of manufacturing concerns. The economic rationale, however, was different. European trading companies were essentially a combination of merchant capitals and entrepreneurs with the blessings of their imperial mother countries. On the other hand, Japanese trading companies were born out of the need to consolidate trading activities in the hands of specialized companies, thereby overcoming Japan's shortage of foreign language ability and trade expertise. As a result of their economic impetus, Japanese trading companies grew rapidly in both size and scope of products and markets covered, into the companies we see today. The largest European trading companies that have survived, for example The East Asiatic Company of Denmark, do not show annual exports valued at more than $1 billion. The largest Japanese *sogo-shosha*, such as Mitsubishi Corporation and Mitsui & Co., show an annual turnover of $60 billion or more, while the smallest *sogo-shosha*'s turnovers are in the $15-20 billion range.

The Japanese *sogo-shosha* are by far the most developed of today's trading companies. The phrase "from missiles to noodles," frequently used to describe the characteristics of *sogo-shosha*, indicates the breadth of their product diversity. An extensive marketing network of over 100 overseas branch offices by each *sogo-shosha* attests to their geographical spread. The fundamental source of strength of *sogo-shosha*, however, is not simply in a summation of products and markets, but in a multiplicative synergy effect derived through functionally integrated operations, such as transportation, distribution, insurance, financing and information gathering. Financing and information gathering, in particular, provide a vital link to business opportunities that would not be viable if pursued independently.

Sogo-shosha did not enjoy the benefits of such diversification from their inception. As outlined in figure 1-1, Japanese trading companies emerged in the late nineteenth century primarily as importers, whose mission was to counter domination by European traders'.[14] Japanese companies accomplished their mission by increasing their share of the import market from 4.7 percent in 1876 to 12.5 percent in 1887, 39.7 percent in 1900, and more than 80 percent by 1918.[15] Having established their position in the domestic market, these trading companies followed Japan's imperialism abroad, expanding their operations to Korea, Manchuria, and Southeast Asian countries in the first half of the twentieth century.

At the end of World War II, General Headquarters of the Supreme Commander of the Allied Powers dismantled the concentration of wealth held by a score of large business groups called *zaibatsu*, on the dubious ground

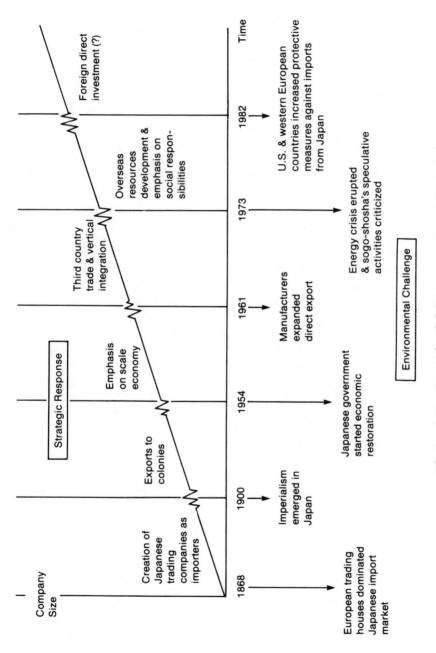

Figure 1-1. Growth of the Japanese *Sogo-Shosha*

that the *zaibatsu* system had been responsible for Japan's imperialistic aggressions abroad and on the more valid ground that such great concentrations of wealth were not conducive to the development of a healthy democratic system at home.[16] Mitsui and Mitsubishi, the prime targets, were broken up into about 250 and 140 independent firms, respectively.[17] For several years afterward each of these companies developed mostly as trading companies specializing in certain product categories. Then under the civilian government in 1954, former Mitsubishi companies were regrouped as Mitsubishi Corporation. Former Mitsui companies regrouped in 1959. These regrouping created trading companies that were substantially larger, stronger, and more sophisticated than before the breakup of the *zaibatsu*. In the interim period, however, a limited number of previously specialized trading companies had filled in the gap created by the dismantling of Mitsui and Mitsubishi, expanding the range of product categories that they covered and becoming *sogo-shosha*. These relative newcomers included traditional textile trading companies called "Five Cotton Traders of the Kansai Area" (C. Itoh, Marubeni, Toyo Menka, Nichimen, Gosho), which took top positions in 1951 exports, as well as a number of metal trading companies such as Ataka and Iwai.[18]

After experiencing phenomenal growth during the 1950s, as a result of the Korean War, *sogo-shosha* entered a period of crisis in the early 1960s. Rapidly growing Japanese manufacturing firms reached a scale economical for handing import and export activities by themselves. The more attractive trade businesses that *sogo-shosha* had, the more likely they were to lose to manufacturers. For the first time, the foundation of *sogo-shosha*'s growth was shaken and their existence threatened. In order to survive, *sogo-shosha* opted for two strategies: third-country trade as a defensive move, and vertical functional integration as an offensive move. First, they moved into third-country trade where they would not be affected by large-scale Japanese manufacturers. At the same time, they developed various trade-related businesses, such as raw-material sourcing, financing, and transportation, which enabled them to gain a competitive edge over the manufacturers and eventually to control them. Although the term *sogo-shosha* first appeared in the late 1950s, it was not until the 1960s that these companies began to benefit from the synergy effect of functional diversification.

Spread of the GTC: Korean GTCs, Taiwanese LTCs, U.S. ETCs

In the early 1970s, the consistent growth of Japanese *sogo-shosha* in the midst of the worldwide economic recession caught the eyes of policymakers in many countries. The governments of developing countries recognized *sogo-shosha* as one of the major causes of the Japanese trade surplus. Soon other countries started to develop their own GTC systems, modeled after the *sogo-shosha*.

The first attempt was made by the Brazilian government, which was concerned with its poor balance-of-payments position. Focusing on exports as the top priority instrument of its industrial policy, the government established Cobec in 1971 and Interbras in 1976. Financing for both companies came from Banco de Brasil, as well as from Brazilian and foreign commercial banks.[19]

In the mid 1970s, Korea's exports experienced a setback from the global recession and the protective trade policies of advanced nations in the wake of the energy crisis. Adding to the problem was overcompetition among small-scale manufacturer-exporters, who did not have expertise in overseas marketing. To regain the fast rate of export growth experienced in the 1960s, the government in 1975 issued an ordinance designating a Korean version of the GTC, called *Chonghap-mooyeok-sangsa*, a direct translation of *sogo-shosha* into Korean. These GTCs were to be large enough to attain economies of scale in the world market, specialized in exportation to gain international competitiveness, and capable of overseas marketing. At the end of 1983, Korea had nine GTCs, which together handled 51.3 percent of Korea's total exports.

The Taiwanese government, noting the apparent success of the Korean GTCs, in 1978 established the *large trading company* (LTC), a modified version of GTC. Unlike the Korean GTC, its objective was twofold: to help promote the nation's exports, and to protect the import market from the hands of foreign traders, especially the Japanese.[20] As of 1984, five large trading companies had been designated by the Taiwanese government, but their combined exports were 1.2 percent of the nation's total. Efforts to establish the GTC system were continued by the governments of Thailand in 1978, the Philippines in 1979 and Turkey in 1980.

The United States, despite an ideology of capitalism based on free competition, was no exception in adopting the GTC system. As a means to ease the problem of increasing trade deficits, President Reagan signed the Export Trading Company (ETC) Act into law in October 1982. Unlike the existing small export management companies (EMCs), which had fragmented services, ETCs were expected to handle multiproduct links with a complete package of export services, so that small- to medium-sized manufacturers, which in the past did not bother to go through the intricacies of exportation, need only go through one step to export their products.

An optimistic view prevailed when the law became a reality; it was expected to create 275,000 jobs and add $22.3 billion to the U.S. GNP.[21] As of June 1984, 349 export trading companies had been formed in the United States. Among them were two pioneers, General Electric Trading Company (GETC) and Sears World Trade Company (SWTC), which had operations based on the extensive overseas networks of the parent corporations. GETC started as a "one-stop export service company,"[22] but it has since focused on countertrade, which has become an indispensable part of G.E.'s business with Eastern bloc and developing countries. SWTC, on the other hand, has aggressively following the concept of a comprehensive export service company; within two years it established 42 offices in 15 countries with 1,000 employees.[23]

Conclusion

With this worldwide spread of GTC systems, it is time to establish a general theory of the GTC, instead of taking the traditional approach of documenting a particular GTC within a specific country and time. The historic analysis presented here provides a set of guidelines for prospective researchers into the subject.

First, the definition of GTC should be made independent from that of the MNC. History proves that the GTC is neither a premature form of the MNC nor its derivative. Therefore, previous attempts to define the GTC, such as, "the GTC will not become an MNC,"[24] or, "the GTC is a Japan-specific MNC"[25] need to be reexamined.

Second, the development of the GTC needs to be studied in conjunction with the trade policy of respective governments. History shows that the GTC was in many countries a product of a government policy designed to overcome the trade barriers of protectionist importing countries.

The third point is a corollary of the second. The management objective of the GTC needs to be understood as different from that of the MNC or other privately held business organizations. Although GTCs are privately held in most countries, their objectives include nationalistic motives strongly influenced by government policies. For instance, their management effectiveness is judged, both within the firm as well as outside, more by export volume than by sheer profitability. Accordingly, the performance of the GTC needs to be measured differently from that of other privately held companies, including the MNC.

Notes

1. Ramkrishna Mukherjee, *The Rise and Fall of the East India Company, A Sociological Approach* (Berlin: VEB Deutscher Verlag der Wissenschaften, 1958), 24.

2. Ibid., 59.

3. James Mill, *The History of British India* (London: James Madden, 1958), 29, in Mukherjee, *The Rise and Fall of the East India Company*, 91.

4. Francis E. Hyde, *Far Eastern Trade 1860–1914* (London: Adam & Charles Black, 1973), 1.

5. Ibid., 9.

6. Kristofer Glamann, *Dutch-Asiatic Trade, 1620–1740* (Copenhagen: Danish Science Press, 1958), 14.

7. Mukherjee, *The Rise and Fall of the East India Company*, 349-350.

8. Edwin Reischauer, *Japan, The Story of a Nation* (revised edition) (New York: Alfred A. Knopf, 1974), 93-95.

9. Dietmar Rothermund, *Asian Trade And European Expansion in the Age of Mercantilism* (New Delhi: Manohar Publishers, 1981), 70.

10. Reischauer, *Japan*, 123.

11. Ibid., 121.

12. Ibid., 130.

13. Yoshihara Kunio, *Sogo Shosha: The Vanguard of the Japanese Economy* (Tokyo: Oxford University Press, 1982), 14-85.

14. In contrast, the Korean government in 1975 allowed the establishment of GTCs as a means of increasing exports.

15. Korea Exchange Bank, *Japanese General Trading Company: Function and Organization* (Seoul: Research Document B-61, 1979), 10.

16. Reischauer, *Japan*, 229.

17. Yoshihara, *Sogo Shosha*, 99.

18. Ibid., 103.

19. Yoshi Tsurumi, *Sogoshosha, Engines of Export-Based Growth* (Montreal: The Institute for Research on Public Policy, 1980), 60-67.

20. Dong-Sung Cho, "The Sogo Shosha Transplanted," *Euro-Asia Business Review* (July 1985):29.

21. "Export Trading Companies," *Chemical Week* (June 27, 1984):92.

22. "A Costly Startup for Sears World Trade," *International Management* (September, 1984):8.

23. Philip Maher, "Trading Companies: A U.S. Export Panacea?" *Industrial Marketing* (October 1982):62.

24. Michael Y. Yoshino, *Japan's Multinational Enterprises* (Cambridge, Mass.: Harvard University Press, 1976), 95.

25. Japanese scholars such as Fujiwara Masao have advocated that the Japanese GTC is a new Japan-style MNC. See Isoda Keiichiro, *Japan-USA Trade and Direct Investment in USA* (Yamakuchi University, Academy of Economics, 1981), 76.

2
The Concept of the General Trading Company

T he questions that immediately arise from the historical analysis in chapter 1 concern the unique characteristic of the GTC. What are the similarities and differences among the various kinds of trading organizations, and specifically, what is the distinguishing feature of the GTC? What economic rationale makes the GTC a superior form of trading organization? This chapter attempts to provide answers to these fundamental questions.

First, we will identify the unique features of the GTC by making a cross-sectional comparison of the diversification strategies of four groups of trading firms—the European trading houses, the Japanese *sogo-shosha*, the Korean general trading companies, and the leading U.S. exporters—in terms of three dimensions: product, geographic, and functional diversification. This will be done by developing appropriate indexes for each kind of diversification strategy and plotting them on a scatter diagram to see the emerging pattern. This quantitative analysis will lead to the conceptual definition of the GTC as any trading company that generates synergy through internal cooperation and coordination of its various business units, which are diversified along product, area, and/or function.

Second, we will examine the various economic advantages that the GTC enjoys through its diversification strategy in comparison to the specialized trading firm. This is elaborated by deductive reasoning, applying such concepts as bounded rationality, information impactedness, and opportunistic behavior to the GTC context.

Finally, we will conclude by reassessing our previously derived model of the GTC and exploring the appropriate growth models that other international business concerns may follow.

Diversification Strategies of Trading Companies

Before arriving at the conceptual definition of the GTC by means of quantitative analysis, we must first make an operational definition of the term *diversification*, develop indexes for each kind of diversification, and select the appropriate sample of firms suitable for our study.

Definition of Diversification Strategies

For most business concerns, diversification is a major strategy for growth. Many researchers have attempted to develop a general theory of diversification, but each has defined diversification according to his or her research goals and methods.

These definitions can be grouped into three paradigms according to the scope of diversification considered. In the first, diversification is treated as an outcome of simultaneous expansion in products and markets; this view is shared by Ansoff,[1] Kinugasa,[2] and Keegan.[3] In the second paradigm, diversification is classified as vertical (dominant-business), horizontal (related-business), and conglomerate (unrelated-business), according to the nature of products being diversified; this view is shared by Stopford and Wells,[4] Rumelt,[5] and Salter and Weinhold.[6] The third view includes functions as well as products and markets; this concept is espoused by Park,[7] Akino,[8] and me in my previous work.[9] Figure 2-1 compares the three paradigms schematically.

The first paradigm, which views diversification as an outcome of interaction between a firm's production capabilities and market conditions, is inadequate for our purpose in this study for the following reasons: (1) it does not readily allow systematic analysis of the many directions and forms of diversification available as a strategy for growth; (2) in practice, managers recognize the difference between geographic and product diversification, and pursue them independently; and (3) it does not provide managers with alternatives for overall growth or organization strategies.

The second paradigm regards the manufacturing of a certain product as the center of a business activity, and then shows how it can be diversified. This paradigm is appropriate for manufacturing firms engaged primarily in production and marketing. However, it largely ignores the strategic needs of business firms operating principally in the service sector.

For the purpose of this study, the third model seems to be the most appropriate. This is particularly true for the GTCs for which functional diversification is an increasingly important element of overall strategy. The resilience of a GTC depends, for example, on its information-gathering capabilities—its ability to locate and match suppliers and buyers in the elusive environment of international business—and on its ability to reduce its exchange-rate exposure by balancing exports and imports.

Choice of Diversification Indexes

Using the third paradigm for defining diversification, let us determine the proxy variables that can be used to measure the degrees of diversification along product, area, and function.

Product Diversification Index (PDI). Various indexes, such as the Herfindahl Index, indicate the degree of product diversification. (See appendix A for

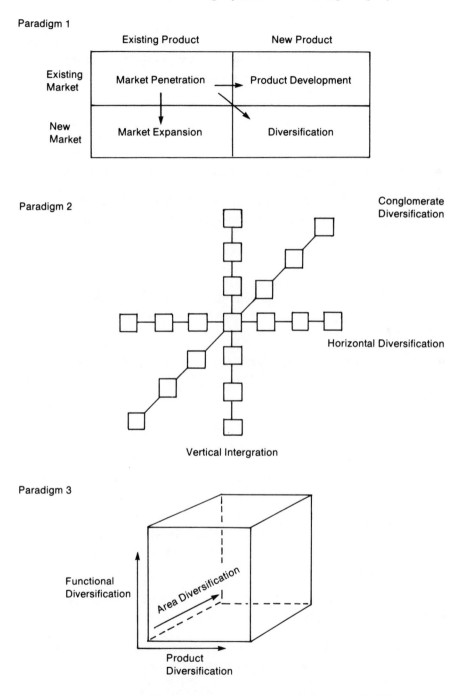

Figure 2-1. Three Paradigms for Defining Diversification

a detailed discussion of various indexes.) However, most of these indexes require detailed information about sales by each product category. Therefore, the Product Diversification Index used for this study is a simpler version developed by Stopford and Wells.[10] It is defined as:

$$\text{PDI} = n \cdot S$$

where

n = number of SIC two-digit industries[11] represented in the product line of the firm, and

S = proportion of total sales generated by products outside the primary product category of the firm.

The boundary value of PDI is 1. Product diversity is defined as low when PDI lies between 0 and 1 ($0 < \text{PDI} < 1$). Similarly, product diversity is defined as high when PDI is greater than 1 ($\text{PDI} > 1$). For a known value of n, the minimum value of S to satisfy the definition of high product diversity can be calculated. For example, if $n = 4$ for a firm with relatively high product diversity, its S must be greater than 0.25.

Area Diversification Index (ADI). Area diversification can also be measured by various indexes. The Area Diversification Index used for this study is defined as:

$$\text{ADI} = 2 \sum_{j=1}^{n} (j \cdot Aj) - 1$$

where

n = 7 (the number of continents), and

Aj = proportion of the number of countries where the firm has branch offices to the total number of countries in the jth continent ($Aj > A_{j+1}$).

Therefore ADI is derived by determining the number of countries entered among the seven continents.

Functional Diversification Index (FDI). International business concerns are so diverse that hasty generalizations about their functions are dangerous and in some cases impossible. Therefore, it is important to delineate the limits of a firm's functional activities before functional diversification can be gauged.

In this context functional activities have been classified to include the following twelve: manufacturing, trade, distribution, finance and investment, insurance, transportation, warehousing, extraction, technical service, leasing, construction, and leisure.

The Functional Diversification Index (FDI) used in this study is calculated by counting the number of functional activities conducted by the firm.

FDI = number of functional activities conducted by the firm.

Selection of Firms for Quantitative Analysis

To measure the degree of diversification of the four groups of traders with the indexes defined above, I selected a sample of companies representative of European trading houses, Japanese *sogo-shosha*, Korean GTCs and U.S. exporters.

The choice of samples for Japanese and Korean GTCs was simple. The following nine Japanese trading companies are commonly referred to as *sogo-shosha*: Mitsubishi Shoji, Mitsui Bussan, C. Itoh, Marubeni, Sumitomo Shoji, Nissho-Iwai, Toyo Menka, Kanematsu-Gosho, and Nichimen, in the order of their turnovers in 1983.[12] As of the end of 1983, nine private companies in Korea received the GTC designation from the Korean government. They are Daewoo Corporation, Samsung Co, Ltd., Hyundai Corporation, Sunkyong Ltd., Bando Sangsa Co. (now Lucky Goldstar International Corporation), Kukje Corporation, Ssangyong Corporation, Hyosung Corporation, and Kumho & Co., in the order of their turnovers in 1983.[13] Thus, all Japanese and Korean GTCs were examined in this study.

On the other hand, defining current European trading houses was difficult, and the necessary data were not readily available. In this study, we are only interested in the trading companies with their roots stemming from the imperial days of Europe. However, most of the traditional trading houses that had prospered in the past either went into oblivion, or were merged into big conglomerates or holding companies, leaving little sign of their existence.[14] Dun & Bradstreet International annually publishes the top 2,500 exporters in Europe, but the list is arbitrary at best because it does not even include the export figures of the companies listed.[15] Therefore, I had to choose the European trading companies on an ad hoc basis. The results were two English companies (Inchcape, the Dunlop Holding ple), one Hong Kong-based English company (Jardine Matheson), two Dutch companies (Internatio-Mueller NV, Ceteco), one Danish company (The East Asiatic Company), and three French companies (OPTORG, SCOA, and CFAO).

Defining the U.S. exporters was an even more difficult task, because definitions of the U.S. exporting firms vary as widely as researchers and authorities in the field.[16] Some argue that export management companies are the most authentic form of exporting companies, but these companies are intermediaries, not fully blown trading companies conducting trading businesses under their own names. Others consider large-sized commodity and raw-material dealers such as Cargill and Phibro as the most advanced exporters. But since these companies are either privately held or part of a holding company, gaining access to data concerning them was very difficult. Probably the most desirable set of companies for this study is the export trading companies (ETCs) based on the Export Trading Company Act of 1982. As of 1983, however, it was premature to consider them a sample representative of U.S. exporters in comparison with the European, the Japanese, and the Korean trading companies chosen above. Given the circumstances, I selected the nine largest U.S. exporters from the list of *Fortune*'s "50 Leading Exporters" as of 1983.[17] They were General Motors, Ford Motor, General Electric, United Technologies, du Pont, IBM, Chrysler, Caterpillar Tractor, and Eastman Kodak in the order of export amounts. Even though Boeing and McDonnell Douglas were originally among the top nine exporters, they had to be excluded because of insufficient data. Instead the tenth and eleventh ranked, Caterpillar Tractor and Eastman Kodak, were included. This list, however, was not without flaws, as the companies chosen also represented multinational corporations based in the United States. Therefore, the inclusion of the leading U.S. exporters in the study should be considered simply for comparison with the trading companies of Europe, Japan, and Korea, without assuming that the U.S. exporters are trading-oriented companies.

Quantitative Analysis of the Diversification
Level of Traders

Product Diversification. As shown in table 2-1, the value of PDI for U.S. exporters ranges between 0.04 and 2.85 with an average of 0.92. With the exception of du Pont, all of the firms have values not exceeding 2.00, indicating a relatively low product diversity. In comparison, the PDIs for the European trading houses lie between 2.08 and 6.42 with an average of 5.14, indicating a generally higher level of diversification than is shown by U.S. exporters. All of the nine Japanese *sogo-shosha* demonstrate a high product diversity, with a PDI concentrated between 6.72 and 7.78 with an average of 7.21. Korean GTCs have also achieved a relatively high product diversity, with a PDI ranging between 3.00 and 6.98 with an average of 5.37. As a group, Korean GTCs show greater product diversification than European trading houses, but less than their Japanese counterparts.

These initial observations are presented diagrammatically in figure 2-2. The figure clearly shows that each of the four international business forms has

Table 2-1
Product Diversification Indexes of
Trading Firms

	PDI
U.S. Exporters	0.92
General Motors	0.28
Ford Motor	0.45
General Electric	2.00
United Technologies	1.56
Du Pont	2.85
IBM	0.04
Chrysler	0.32
Caterpillar Tractor	0.18
Eastman Kodak	0.60
European Trading Houses	5.14
CFAO	5.25
SCOA	5.71
OPTORG	4.72
Internatio-Mueller	5.60
Inchcape	6.18
Dunlop	2.08
CETECO	N.A.
East-Asiatic Co.	6.42
Jardine Matheson	N.A.
Japanese Sogo-Shosha	7.21
Mitsubishi Shoji	7.19
Mitsui Bussan	7.36
C. Itoh	6.72
Marubeni	7.52
Sumitomo Shoji	7.78
Nissho-Iwai	7.12
Toyo Menka	7.46
Kanematsu-Gosho	6.97
Nichimen	6.80
Korean GTCs	5.37
Samsung	6.94
Daewoo	4.82
Hyundai	3.00
Lucky-Gold Star	5.50
Ssangyong	5.30
Sunkyong	5.26
Hyosung	6.98
Kukje	5.14
Kumho	N.A.

achieved a distinctive level of product diversity. For example, it can be seen that U.S. exporters are far less diversified from a product standpoint than the other three groups of trading companies, while the Japanese *sogo-shosha* are the most diversified. These interesting findings provide some solid empirical

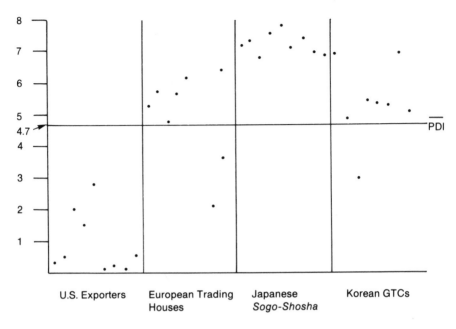

Figure 2-2. Graph of Product Diversification Index for Trading Companies

evidence in support of the hypothesis on product diversification that we will discuss in the next section.

Area Diversification. Area diversification expressed by ADI is presented in table 2-2. The average value of ADI is highest for the Japanese *sogo-shosha*, at 5.23. The average value for U.S. exporters is somewhat lower at 4.11, and even lower for Korean GTCs at 3.59. The average value of ADI is lowest for the European trading houses, at 2.81. As can be seen more clearly from the diagram in figure 2-3, Japanese *sogo-shosha* have achieved the most extensive area diversification and the European trading houses the least, with the U.S. exporters and Korean GTCs falling in between.

Functional Diversification. To determine the extent of a firm's functional diversification, I primarily relied on the articles of incorporation of each firm, and considered only those activities that were specifically mentioned. The information compiled is presented in table 2-3 and figure 2-4. Japanese *sogo-shosha* show a consistently high level of functional diversification, participating in eight to eleven activities. As a group, Korean GTCs show the most limited degree of functional diversification, two to six. The U.S. exporters and

Table 2-2
Area Diversification Indexes of
Trading Firms

	ADI
U.S. Exporters	4.11
General Motors	4.09
Ford Motor	3.55
General Electric	5.00
United Technologies	4.00
Du Pont	3.62
IBM	4.31
Chrysler	3.80
Caterpillar Tractor	4.44
Eastman Kodak	4.17
European Trading Houses	2.81
CFAO	1.72
SCOA	2.41
OPTORG	1.17
Internatio-Mueller	3.16
Inchcape	4.31
Dunlop	3.84
CETECO	2.42
East-Asiatic Co.	3.76
Jardine Matheson	2.56
Japanese Sogo-Shosha	5.23
Mitsubishi Shoji	5.60
Mitsui Bussan	5.44
C. Itoh	6.06
Marubeni	5.44
Sumitomo Shoji	5.51
Nissho-Iwai	5.43
Toyo Menka	4.81
Kanematsu-Gosho	4.52
Nichimen	4.24
Korean GTCs	3.59
Samsung	4.23
Daewoo	3.62
Hyundai	3.27
Lucky-Gold Star	3.37
Ssangyong	3.38
Sunkyong	4.18
Hyosung	3.64
Kukje	3.00
Kumho	N.A.

European trading houses are similar in that they fall in between, but their mode of functional diversification is quite different. U.S. exporters are generally diversified into distribution, financing, insurance, and other functions to support their sales efforts, while the European trading houses have achieved

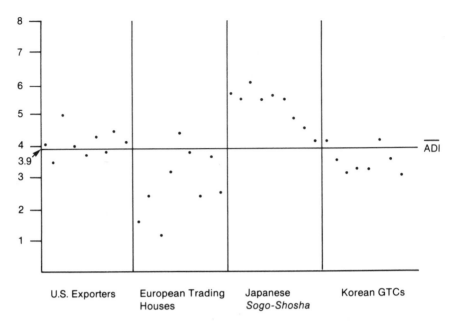

Figure 2-3. Graph of Area Diversification Index for Trading Companies

their functional diversification by operating independent business entities, rather than support functions, in the local economies.

Definition of the General Trading Company

We have examined the commonalities and differences among four forms of trading companies in terms of three kinds of diversification—product, geographic area and function. The quantitative analysis provides empirical evidence about the nature of these trading concerns, summarized in table 2-4. The table shows that each type of firm has achieved a different degree of diversification.

European trading houses are diversified by product and function but not by area. These firms originally focused their operations on regions in which their governments historically enjoyed significant political influence. Therefore, their geographic diversification was generally limited to colonies. Efforts to maximize economic exploitation of the colonies, however, served to promote both product and functional diversification. European trading houses engaged fully in two-way trade, importing raw materials and products from the colonies while exporting manufactured goods in return. Profits were

Table 2-3
Functional Diversification Indexes of
Trading Firms

	FDI
U.S. Exporters	6.4
General Motors	7
Ford Motor	5
General Electric	7
United Technologies	5
Du Pont	6
IBM	8
Chrysler	8
Caterpillar Tractor	7
Eastman Kodak	5
European Trading Houses	8.3
CFAO	9
SCOA	9
OPTORG	8
Internatio-Mueller	6
Inchcape	11
Dunlop	5
CETECO	8
East-Asiatic Co.	10
Jardine Matheson	9
Japanese Sogo-Shosha	9.6
Mitsubishi Shoji	11
Mitsui Bussan	10
C. Itoh	10
Marubeni	10
Sumitomo Shoji	9
Nissho-Iwai	9
Toyo Menka	9
Kanematsu-Gosho	8
Nichimen	10
Korean GTCs	4.5
Samsung	4
Daewoo	5
Hyundai	4
Lucky-Gold Star	6
Ssangyong	2
Sunkyong	4
Hyosung	5
Kukje	6
Kumho	N.A.

increased further by controlling every stage of the trade, from extraction of natural resources and cultivation to collection, transportation, and marketing.

Japanese *sogo-shosha* are diversified in all three dimensions. Their earliest activities, in the 1870s and 1880s, were designed to form a common front

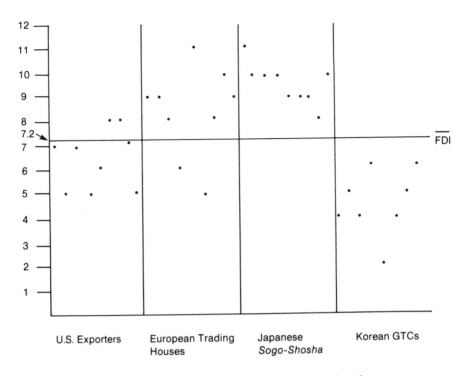

Figure 2-4. Graph of Functional Diversification Index for Trading Companies

against European trading houses penetrating the Japanese market. In the late nineteenth and the early twentieth centuries, they expanded to various Japanese colonies. Compared with typical European trading houses, which also depended on the colonies of their home countries but generally specialized in specific areas, Japanese trading companies were fewer in number and larger in size, thus able to move into multiple markets simultaneously.[18] In the 1960s and 1970s, many Japanese manufacturing companies attained sufficient scale to go abroad themselves. Threatened with this development, Japanese trading companies developed various functional activities such as raw-material sourcing, financing, transportation, and information gathering, to enable them to keep the smaller sized manufacturers under control.[19]

Through various requirements, the Korean government mandated a considerable product and geographic diversity for its GTCs.[20] Functional diversification other than export activities, however, has not been emphasized. As a result, Korean GTCs show only a limited functional diversification into importation or third-country trade. Similarly, finance, information services, and transportation play relatively minor roles in their modes of operation.

Table 2-4
Diversification Strategies of Trading Firms

Diversification	Korean GTCs	European Trading Houses	U.S. Traders	Japanese GTCs
Product	Yes	Yes	No	Yes
Area	Yes	No	Yes	Yes
Function	No	Yes	Yes	Yes

The leading U.S. exporters, which are essentially U.S.-based MNCs, specialize in a limited line of products based on extensive research and development, the traditional source of U.S. comparative advantage. In area and function, on the other hand, U.S. exporters are widely diversified. For example, General Motors is engaged almost exclusively in the production and sale of passenger cars and other motor vehicles, but has a worldwide marketing network in over 30 countries. Furthermore, in each market, General Motors conducts numerous functional activities, such as production of parts, assembly, after-service, and consumer financing.

Based on these findings, we can now construct a schematic model of the diversification strategies of the different trading companies. The result is a hexahedron, shown in figure 2-5, whose corners show the degrees and directions of diversification. Korean GTCs are represented by the point E, suggesting that they are diversified by product and area but not by function. European trading houses, represented by point F, are diversified by product and function but not by area. U.S. exporters, at point G, are diversified by area and function but not by product. Japanese GTCs, at point H, are fully diversified in product, area and function.[21]

From this model we can find the following commonality among the four groups of traders: Each of the four groups is diversified by at least two dimensions. If we regard all of Japanese, European, and Korean trading companies as GTCs, the necessary condition of the GTC would be to diversify along more than one dimension among product, area, and function. Indeed, this condition is necessary for any company to generate a positive synergy effect, that is, to have the sum of its output greater than that of its imput. In this context, Japanese *sogo-shosha* is undoubtedly the most developed form of the GTC.

Nevertheless, this condition alone does not guarantee that a company will function like a GTC, because the synergy effect is not automatically derived from the business structure of a company itself. For a company to generate the synergy effect, it must purposefully manage the various product, area, or functional segments within the company so that the coordination of these segments results in more than what the segments create individually. Therefore, to be qualified as a full-fledged GTC, a trading company must generate synergy through internal cooperation and coordination of its various business units, which are diversified along product, area, and/or function.

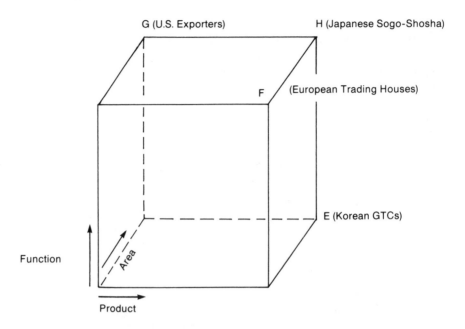

Figure 2-5. Diversification Strategies for Trading Companies

The Economic Rationale of the GTC's Diversification

We have just shown that the four groups of trading companies can be distinguished from one another by the degrees of diversification in product, area, and function, and that Japanese *sogo-shosha* are the most diversified among the four groups compared. Now let us consider the reasons why diversification is more advantageous than nondiversification when a trading company tries to increase its export volume. We will analyze the economic rationale of the GTC's diversification by means of deductive reasoning.

According to our definition of the GTC, its characteristics lie in its diversification along multiple dimensions. Therefore, we need to prove the advantages of diversification along multiple dimensions, in order to prove that the GTC is a superior form of business compared to specialized trading companies or trading companies diversified along only one dimension. This can be done by proving the following two postulates:

1. Diversified trading companies are more advantageous than specialized trading companies when they seek for trading opportunities.
2. Diversified trading companies along multiple dimensions are more advantageous than diversified trading companies along a single dimension when they seek for trading opportunities.

The first postulate needs to be subdivided into three cases according to the directions of diversification, because of the fundamental differences among product, area, and functional diversification. The second postulate must take into account the effect of synergy.

Product Diversification

The literature discusses in depth the benefits of conglomeration to a manufacturing concern, which is roughly equivalent to product diversification of a trading company. For example, Alfred Chandler demonstrated various causes and effects of product diversification through the example of du Pont in his pioneering book *Strategy and Structure*.[22] A more comprehensive evaluation of the effects of product diversification was attempted by Dennis Mueller,[23] Igor Ansoff,[24] and Salter and Weinhold,[25] who identified increased market power, reduced risks, increased price-earning ratio, more efficient cash management through capital redeployment, reduced costs of debt capital, and growth in profits through cross-subsidization as the benefits of such diversification.

A manager's decision to diversify products, however, is not only affected by expectations of benefits, but is also constrained by a manager's own perception of what he or she can and cannot do. In this respect, the concept of bounded rationality can be used to explain the reason for product diversification. According to Herbert Simon, bounded rationality is a human behavior that is "intendedly rational, but only limitedly so."[26] It refers to the limitations of future uncertainty and insufficient knowledge of complicated problems that a human being faces in making decisions.[27]

A trading company that is specialized in trading a single product is, by definition, limited in knowledge to that particular product. Even when the product is distributed extensively worldwide, and when this company has an intensive knowledge about each of its markets, it is not likely to try to seek an opportunity in these markets for other attractive products. This limitation is due to its bounded rationality, that is, its preoccupation with the product in which it is specialized.

This limitation does not handicap the efficiency of the specialized company's operation, as long as the sales volume of the single product is large enough to fully employ company resources. If the volume is less than the level at which the company can fully utilize its resources, the efficiency of the operation is lower. Thus when a trading company handles a large volume of a single product, it can afford to specialize in this product. On the other hand, when a single product does not provide enough volume, the company will have to diversify its product lines.

Area Diversification

In the case of a trading company specializing in a specific geographic area, the rationality of its managers is bounded by their territorial concern, beyond which their understanding is limited. Opportunities in other parts of the world are not easily materialized. Bounded rationality has indeed become one of the major criteria used to differentiate between the domestic corporation and the international corporation. For example, Perlmutter coined the phrase "ethnocentric perspective" to describe the bounded rationality of management in a domestically oriented company, in comparison with "polycentric" and "geocentric" perspectives of management in multinational and global corporations, respectively.[28]

The limitation of an area-specialized trading company can also be explained by the concept of information impactedness, which is a result of the firm's acting only in its own territory. According to Oliver Williamson, information impactedness is a condition in which "true underlying circumstances relevant to the transaction, or related set of transactions, are known to one or more parties but cannot be costlessly discerned by or displayed for others."[29] This condition is the result of either bounded rationality of the management, or internal limits such as cost or time of the company. When such a circumstance prevails, information in various regional markets is not perfectly distributed among trading companies with different degrees of involvement. The trading company that has internalized a certain regional market by establishing branch offices and accumulating business contacts through them generally has better access to information than the trading company without such an internal market. It is thus able to attain more business opportunities and better operating results.

Functional Diversification

Functional diversification in a trading company results in vertical integration. The company that starts as a trader may integrate backward into manufacturing the product that it has traded, and into resources development and importation to supply manufacturers with necessary raw materials. It can also integrate forward into transportation and warehousing, insurance, and other trade-related businesses.

The advantages of a functionally diversified trading company can be easily derived from the merits of vertical integration, such as stabilization of supply and demand between adjoining businesses, and the effect of forming an entry barrier to potential competitors. A more fundamental source of these advantages, however, is that they avoid opportunistic behavior by parties engaged in business with trading companies. Opportunistic behavior is a false threat or promise for the purpose of individual advantage.[30] Strategic manipulation of information, or misrepresentation of intentions, are examples of opportunistic behavior by a firm expecting to gain a competitive advantage over other companies in the industry.[31]

Opportunistic behavior restricts the opportunities of a trading company engaged only in proper trading business. An independent trading company may try to develop a new trading opportunity abroad for a manufacturing company that is affiliated with a trading company or has a trading division within its corporation. In this circumstance, the independent trader must take into account the possibility of opportunistic behavior by the manufacturing company, which may not fully disclose the information needed. On the other hand, an internal trader would not face opportunistic behavior by the manufacturing company, either because of access to internal information sources that outsiders may not have, or because of the cooperative atmosphere within the corporation.

The internal trader has an advantage to the extent that the transaction partners within the same corporation are not structured as autonomous business units with competing accountability, causing intraorganization rivalry. In this case, internal organization substitutes the external market as a place where arms-length transactions take place. This phenomenon, called "internalization" by industrial economists, explains the advantage that a functionally diversified—and thus vertically integrated—trading company has over a trading company with a limited scope of trading activities.[32]

Multidimensional Diversification

The GTC is diversified in various dimensions simultaneously. Multidimensional diversification can be subdivided into four combinations: product and area, area and function, function and product, and product and area and function. Although the rationale of each of these diversifications can be explored separately,[33] the term *synergy* may be used to explain them as a common denominator.

Synergy is commonly used to describe the process that causes the sum of an output to be greater than that of its input.[34] We can deduce the positive effect of synergy from diversification through a simple numerical illustration. Consider a hypothetical company X, which needs 1 unit of management resources to develop a product, 1 unit to find a market, and 1 unit to engage in exports, thereby achieving $1 \times 1 \times 1 = 1$ unit in sales. For X, $1 + 1 + 1 = 3$ units of management resources are required for 1 unit in sales, and therefore, X's initial productivity per unit of management resources is $1/3$. If X expands its market by employing another unit of management resources, it would be able to produce $1 \times 2 \times 1 = 2$ units in sales by employing $1 + 2 + 1 = 4$ units of management resources, increasing unit productivity to $2/4$, or $1/2$.

If the next unit of management resources is employed toward area diversification, the result would be $1 \times 3 \times 1 = 3$ units in sales. In contrast, if employed toward product diversification, $2 \times 2 \times 1 = 4$ units in sales would be produced. Similarly, the next available unit of management resources can be most effectively employed toward functional diversification. If it is so employed, X would achieve $2 \times 2 \times 2 = 8$ units in sales, compared to $3 \times 2 \times 1 = 6$ units in sales that would result from further product diversification.

By pursuing diversification in all three directions, Japanese *sogo-shosha* were able to maximize the synergy effect. As a result, *sogo-shosha*, despite their initial backwardness in technology and lack of experience, maintained a generally higher level of growth in exports than U.S. exporters and European trading houses in the post-World-War-II period.

Japanese *sogo-shosha* are the most complete form of the GTC, according to our definition. This is not to suggest that *sogo-shosha* are perfect as a generic form of the GTC from a theoretical point of view, or that *sogo-shosha* are the only acceptable form of the GTC. Other trading firms, especially Korean and European trading companies, also enjoy a high level of synergy effects through multiple directions of diversification. By defining the GTC as the large-scale trading companies that have achieved diversification in at least two directions, we can include European trading houses and Korean GTCs as two alternative forms of the GTC.

Notes

1. H. Igor Ansoff, *Corporate Strategy, Business Policy for Growth and Expansion* (New York: McGraw-Hill Book Company, 1965), 128.

2. Yo'oske Kinugasa, *Internationalization Strategy of Japanese Enterprise* (Tokyo: Nihon Keizai Shimposha, 1979), 46, 49.

3. Warren J. Keegan, "Strategic Marketing: International Diversification Versus National Concentration," *Columbia Journal of World Business* (Winter 1977).

4. John A. Stopford and Louis T., Wells, Jr., *Managing the Multinational Enterprise* (New York: Basic Books, Inc., 1972), 36-38.

5. Richard P. Rumelt, *Strategy, Structure, and Economic Performance*, Division of Research, Harvard University Graduate School of Business Administration, 1974, 9-31.

6. Malcolm S. Salter and Wolf A. Weinhold, *Diversification through Acquisition* (New York: The Free Press, 1979), 6-7.

7. Je-Ka Park, *Bookhakeui*, translated by Ik-Sung Lee (Seoul: Eulyoo Moonhwasa, 1974).

8. Norihiro Akino, "Quantitative Analysis of Trading Companies' Diversification Activities," (I) and (II), *Kannan Keiei*, 1978 and 1979.

9. Dong-Sung Cho, *Hankook-eui Chonghap Muyuk Sangsa: Bonjil-kwa Jeon-ryak* (Korea's General Trading Company: Concept and Strategy) (Bupmoonsa, 1983), 84.

10. Stopford and Wells, *Managing the Multinational Enterprise*, 185-187.

11. Standard industry classification differs from country to country. Therefore, a reclassification of industry data was necessary for international comparisons.

12. This listing is not unanimous. Some sources consider only the largest six as full-fledged *sogo-shosha*, while the Sogo Shosha Committee of the Japan Trade Council, Inc. is composed of sixteen companies that include the above nine plus Chori, Itoman, Kawasho, Kinsho-Mataichi, Nozaki, Okura, and Toshoku.

13. As of 1983, there were ten GTCs in Korea. One of them, Koryo Trading Co., is under the control of the Korea Trade Promotion Corporation (KOTRA) and responsible for fostering export activities of small and medium manufacturers in Korea. Koryo Trading was, therefore, excluded from our analysis. In 1984, the Korean government excluded Kumho from the Korean GTCs because of its failure to meet the mandated requisites, thus maintaining nine companies altogether. Since the data used in this book were as of the end of 1983 in most cases, we will define the Korean GTCs with nine companies which include Kumho but exclude Koryo.

14. East India Companies in various countries have all disappeared, while many colony-based trading companies are now part of big conglomerates. For example, Dodwell Company is now a wholly-owned subsidiary of the Inchcape Group, and the United Africa Company is a division of Unilever.

15. *Europe's 10,000 Largest Companies* (London: Dun & Bradstreet International, 1983).

16. The Office of Export Company Affairs, U.S. Department of Commerce, has made no attempt to define the export company because of the variety of differing opinions.

17. "The 50 Leading U.S. Exporters," *Fortune* (August 6, 1984): 37.

18. Until the 1950s, Japanese trading companies exhibited a diversification mode similar to the present-day GTCs in Korea. Operations of trading companies such as Mitsui and Mitsubishi were well diversified in product and in area, but functional activities were very much limited to importing raw materials and exporting manufactured goods.

19. Alexander K. Young, *The Sogo-Shosa: Japan's Multinational Trading Companies* (Boulder, Colo.: Westview Press, 1976), 11-13.

20. Cho, *Hankook-eui Chonghap Muyuk Sangsa*, 20-24.

21. In the hexahedron presented in figure 2-5, point A is the origin, where a business entity has yet to be established. Points B, C and D represent companies that are diversified in only one dimension. A company at point B is diversified in product, but not in area or function; for example, a general merchandise store. A company at point C is diversified in area, but not in product or function; for example, a distributor for a manufacturing firm. A company at point D is diversified in function, but not in area or product; for example, a service center.

22. Alfred D. Chandler, Jr., *Strategy and Structure: Chapters in the History of the American Industrial Enterprise* (Cambridge, Mass.: The M.I.T. Press, 1962), 52-113.

23. Dennis C. Mueller, "A Theory of Conglomerate Mergers," *The Quarterly Journal of Economics* 83(November 1969):643-659.

24. H. Igor Ansoff, *Corporate Strategy—An Analytic Approach to Business Policy for Growth and Expansion* (New York: McGraw-Hill Book Company, 1965), 135-138.

25. Malcolm S. Salter and Wolf A. Weinhold, *Diversification Through Acquisition, Strategies for Creating Economic Value* (New York: The Free Press, 1979), 133-146.

26. Herbert A. Simon, *Administrative Behavior*, 2nd ed. (New York: The Macmillan Company, 1961), xxiv.

27. Oliver E. Williamson, *Markets and Hierarchies: Analysis and Antitrust Implications* (New York: The Free Press, 1975), 22.

28. Heenan, David A., and Perlmutter, Howard V., *Multinational Organization Development* (Reading, Mass.: Addison-Wesley Publishing Company, 1979).

29. Williamson, *Markets and Hierarchies*, 31.

30. Ibid., 26.

31. Michael Porter has developed a framework to make use of the opportunistic behvior in generating competitive strategies. *See* Michael E. Porter, *Competitive Strategy* (New York: Free Press, 1980).

32. The basic concept about market failure that promotes internationalization of transaction was first formulated by Ronald Coase in 1937, then resurrected by Arrow and Williamson. Buckley and Casson applied the concept to the MNC. See Ronald H. Coase, "The Nature of the Firm" *Economica* 4(November 1937); Kenneth J. Arrow, "Vertical Integration and Communication" *Bell Journal of Economics* 5(Spring 1975); Williamson, *Markets and Hierarchies*; Peter J. Buckley and Mark Casson, *The Future of the Multinational Enterprise* (London: The MacMillan Press Ltd., 1976).

33. Regarding product and area diversification, Igor Ansoff uses the term *diversification* when new product development and market expansion take place simultaneously, and explains the reasons why diversification along both product and market is more advantageous than pure conglomerate diversification (product diversification) or market expansion (area diversification). See Ansoff, *Corporate Strategy*, 129-138. Regarding area and functional diversification, Richard Holton identifies as one of the incentives to integrate manufacturing and wholesaling functions the trend that the sale of the manufacturer's product becomes more geographically dense (international). See Richard H. Holton, "The Role of Competition and Monopoly in Distribution: The Experience in the United States," in Lee E. Preston, ed. *Social Issues in Marketing* (Glenview, Ill.: Scott, Foresman and Company, 1968), 151-153.

34. Ansoff, *Corporate Strategy*, 75.

3
The General Trading Company versus the Multinational Corporation

Among the four kinds of trading companies that we have examined, one is more properly labeled multinational corporations, a group of firms to which most of the leading U.S. traders belong. The U.S. multinational corporations have followed an avenue of growth quite different from that of the trading companies of Europe, Japan, and Korea. Their motives for export activities are also quite different. The trading companies of Europe, Japan, and Korea were the products of government policies in their respective countries. They were developed when the government perceived a need for commercial institutions that could help domestic manufacturers introduce their products abroad. In essence, the reason for the GTC lies in its ability to provide domestic manufacturers with expertise in international-business activities by handling for them a large number of products, by penetrating various geographic areas, and by performing multiple facilitative functions. This diversification in products, geographic areas, and/or functions allows the GTC to become a self-sustaining entity with an economical scale, as we have seen most vividly in the case of the Japanese *sogo-shosha*.

U.S.-based multinational corporations, on the other hand, grew primarily by manufacturing a limited number of products and marketing them internationally through their own initiatives and efforts. Businesses that started as single-product, single-function (mostly manufacturing) organizations became multifunctional mostly in the late nineteenth and early twentieth centuries, when they attained a scale enabling them to move forward into marketing and distribution, and then backward into raw- and semifinished-material sourcing and research and development. In the process of moving forward, they invested abroad, first in marketing and then in production, and ultimately became multinational.[1]

Because of their differences in origins and patterns of growth, general trading companies and multinational corporations have pursued different diversification strategies. Their differences lie not only in the number of products covered, but also in other key corporate strategies. This chapter compares the two organizational forms in terms of the strategies they commonly exercise. Strategic issues considered here include the mode of internationalization, the means of external growth, organization, personnel, coordination, finance, and the balance between line functions. To make the comparison substantive, Japanese *sogo-shosha* and U.S.-based multinational corporations are assumed to represent general trading companies and multinational corporations, respectively.

Internationalization Strategy

To U.S. entrepreneurs, a large domestic market initially offered an almost limitless opportunity for expansion. As a result, firms showed very little interest in developing overseas markets until the late nineteenth century, when they found in them an opportunity to sustain high levels of growth.

Traditionally, and especially since the 1950s, the primary strategic concern of U.S. entrepreneurs was to increase their domestic market shares. To increase the price competitiveness of their products, U.S. entrepreneurs aimed at reducing production costs. An excellent opportunity for low-cost production was first found in post-war Europe and Japan, where labor costs were substantially lower than in the United States. When European and Japanese wage levels increased sharply during the 1960s, U.S. firms turned to less-developed countries as a site for low-cost production.[2] U.S. entrepreneurs transferred abroad capital, machinery, and technological expertise, and imported finished goods in return. The result was a substantial increase in foreign direct investment.

In Japan, the limited size of the domestic market constrained entrepreneurs' desire for growth. Japanese traders, therefore, started exploring overseas markets as soon as they controlled the domestic market in the late nineteenth century. They were helped by the expansionary policies of their imperial government, which encouraged firms to increase their exports of finished goods to the colonies.

After World War II, exportation continued to receive active government support. However, the government's goal was more than simply expanding export volumes. Recognizing the need to maintain low production costs to assure future competitiveness in foreign markets, the Japanese government sought ways to reduce the cost of raw material imports. A solution was found in delegating the import rights of raw materials to a limited number of large trading companies, rather than allowing each firm to import its share. Such purchasing rights were given to the *sogo-shosha*. The buying power of the resulting monopsony effectively served to lower import costs, and the *sogo-shosha* came to play an increasingly prominent role in the Japanese economy, both as major exporters of finished goods and as importers of raw materials.

External Growth Strategy

The growth of U.S.-based MNCs can be attributed to both the accumulation of capital through secular sales increases and the concentration of capital through mergers and acquisitions. It was generally the latter that allowed the rapid development of U.S. companies into large-scale MNCs. A recent study, for example, showed that two-thirds of the 100 largest U.S. companies in 1969 were products of mergers and acquisitions.[3]

The series of mergers and acquisitions in the U.S. can be divided into three periods. The first stage, begun in the late nineteenth century, saw horizontally oriented mergers of companies in the same industry. By the 1890s, increased industrial productivity had led to an excess supply of manufactured goods. Faced with surplus capacity and increasingly fierce price competition, U.S. entrepreneurs collaborated among themselves to ensure their profitability. They formed cartels by fixing prices and dividing up the domestic market. Such collusions were soon broken from within, as larger companies found the means to dominate other companies in their industries. Standard Oil, for example, was able to gain effective control over smaller petroleum companies after forming a trust. Subsequently, in 1899, when the revised commercial code in New Jersey allowed the establishment of holding companies, Standard Oil Trust was reorganized into Standard Oil of New Jersey, effecting the legal merger of all related companies under the trust into one giant corporation. Similarly, such mergers allowed U.S. Steel and General Electric to emerge as dominant companies in their respective industries. Three major factors aided mergers in this period: the recessionary business environment, which made smaller companies particularly vulnerable; the completion of the railroad network across the continent, which made geographic expansion more manageable; and an active financial market, which facilitated large-size capital investments.

The second stage of mergers was characterized by vertically oriented acquisitions of companies in related industries. At the end of World War I, U.S. entrepreneurs found themselves with surplus capacities in their war-related industries. They sought diversification as a long-term strategy for growth, and began to pursue both forward and backward integrations. At the same time, they adopted a decentralized management structure, organized by industry segments, and began to expand their overseas operations as part of their diversification strategy.

In the post-World-War-II era conglomerates appeared. U.S. enterprises had accumulated substantial capital during the war period, but the government's stringent enforcement of antitrust laws made it difficult to increase market shares in most industries. Acquiring small- and medium-sized companies in unrelated industries allowed firms to invest their surplus capital and maintain their high levels of growth. This acquisition strategy was facilitated by an active and bullish stock market, which made such investments in securities quite attractive.[4]

Conglomerates, not driven by the traditional goals of achieving economies of scale or market dominance, became decentralized and market-diversified entities, using their management skill and easy access to financial markets. More prone to penetrate small foreign markets, conglomerates acquired local companies within each market, making foreign direct investment an integral part of their overall acquisition strategy. ITT and Litton Industries were foremost among conglomerates pursuing such a global acquisition strategy.

The Japanese economy was traditionally dominated by a handful of large enterprises called *zaibatsu*. At the end of the World War II, the holding companies of these *zaibatsu* were dissolved by the General Headquarters of the Allied Powers. After the restoration of Japanese civilian government, however, former members of *zaibatsu* regrouped, attracted to one another by traditional ties and loyalties, shared values, and the realization that collaboration would lead to increased business opportunities and profits.[5] To compete with the power of former *zaibatsu* group companies, other Japanese firms started pooling their capital resources around major banks such as Dai-Ichi, Fuyo, and Sanwa, creating their own business groups.

Japanese business groups have adopted five basic strategies to strengthen their organizations: (1) each group has a major bank whose role is to channel outside capital to the group; (2) each group has a *sogo-shosha* that acts as both the sales and purchasing agent for the group; (3) each group uses outside banks and trading companies to spread political and economic risks and to take advantage of large-scale transactions, including syndicated loans; (4) each group creates new business units within the group through joint investment and interlocking ownership; and (5) since the early 1970s, each group has established joint ventures with other business groups as well.[6]

The relationships among business units within a Japanese business group and among Japanese business groups themselves are shown in figure 3-1. Banks and *sogo-shosha* are the core units in every Japanese business group. *Sogo-shosha,* in particular, provide the group with an effective information-gathering capacity and an extensive domestic sales network. In return, *sogo-shosha* handle exclusively the sales and purchasing functions of the member companies in the group. They further discover new business opportunities and undertake initial investment for the group in new industries.

A *sogo-shosha* has two major sources of income, the monopoly profit derived from its role as a sales agent, and the risk premium for participating in relatively unknown markets.[7] These profits come from *sogo-shosha's* unique ability to organize business activities. Since a *sogo-shosha's* strength lies in

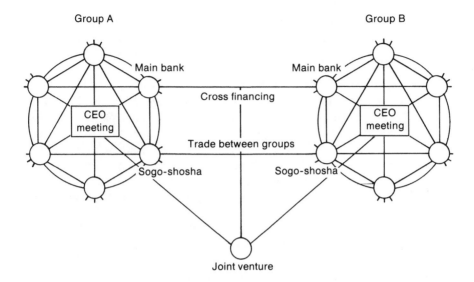

Figure 3-1. Japanese Business-Group Structure

diverse functional capability rather than technology or manufacturing abilities, it must have strong support from manufacturing firms. In doing business abroad, therefore, *sogo-shosha* typically act only as the pathfinder, delegating the major role in foreign direct investment to manufacturing companies inside and outside the group.

Organization Strategy

As we have noted, U.S. enterprises achieved considerable product diversity and geographic expansion through a series of mergers and acquisitions. At the same time, they replaced a centralized, functionally organized management structure with a decentralized one. While in the old structure each unit operated under a specific functional charter, such as sales or production, in the new structure industry segments had both production and sales responsibility for a given range of products.[8]

This transition to a decentralized management structure can be considered simply a creative response to changes in the business environment.[9] It was, however, more than that since the root of a decentralized management can be found in the U.S. social value system. Reassigning decision-making power to a lower level was more suitable in a cultural environment where individual ability and innovativeness were highly valued.

*Sogo-shosha*s appear from the outside to be organized into units with specific product or geographic responsibilities. However, a look at their internal operations reveals that *sogo-shosha* actually emphasize business units by functional specialization and coordination among units to cope with constantly changing markets and consumer demand.

Functional activities of *sogo-shosha* can be divided into main and support functions. Main functions include trade, finance, and information gathering. Support functions include raw-material development, industrial management, and software systems such as project and material management. It is important to note that none of these functions is considered an end in itself. For example, information capabilities are maintained to support trading activities. Similarly, financing capabilities are used to attract small-sized manufacturing firms.

While *sogo-shosha*'s individual functional capabilities display a high degree of sophistication, they all serve to support the company's goal of growth through increased trade activities. *Sogo-shosha* emphasize global maximization of profits rather than internal allocation of profits or the performance of individual units. This is in contrast to the U.S.-based MNCs, which emphasize local maximization of income, with each business unit operating as a separate profit center.

Personnel Strategy

By the late nineteenth century, the United States had become an industrial nation, needing an increased labor force to continue economic growth. To supplement the shortage in local labor supply, the United States increased immigration. This policy of contractual slavery served the country well as long as economic growth continued unabated. However, it led to a major social problem during the economic depression. Many companies started to lay off their workers and some refused to pay wages. The resulting social malaise led to the organization of labor unions.

The resistance of U.S. entrepreneurs to unions was not simply for economic reasons: U.S. entrepreneurs saw unions as both an undesirable partner sharing the profits of their business ventures and a challenge to their right to freely pursue business opportunities.[10] The labor movement was considered a challenge to the right to private property, which is the foundation of capitalism. Given the prospects of having to forego their right to dismissal, U.S. companies turned to short-term employment policies as an alternative.

Although the United States does not have a traditional class structure, Americans are no less class conscious than are members of older societies. In the United States, membership in a specific social circle is often valued more than company loyalty. Since there is no aristocracy or other traditional hierarchy, social distinction is based primarily on income level. Higher income gives Americans not only membership to exclusive social circles but greater independence and comfort. In a society where labor mobility is particularly high, it is inevitable that attractive salary offers are the primary form of inducement for qualified employees.

In Japan, the rapid growth of light industries in the early twentieth century sharply increased the demand for labor, resulting in an intense competition among firms for the limited labor supply and a mass movement of labor from rural to urban areas. However, the acute economic recession at the end of World War I, and eventually the Great Depression, eradicated the bargaining power of labor over management.[11]

Most small- and medium-sized firms reacted to the depression by reducing their work force. In contrast, large companies negotiated with employees to share the burden of the depression, retaining their workforce but reducing wages. Companies that survived the depression made this retention program a permanent part of their policy and the foundation of Japanese labor-management relations. Currently, about one-third of the total labor force works under the benefit of such a life-time employment system, which exists in most large companies, including *sogo-shosha.*

There are two notable elements in this lifetime employment system. First, employees have undefined responsibility. They are not evaluated as individuals, but as members of the work teams to which they belong. Their responsibilities are whatever is necessary for the team to achieve its task. Second, employees' general and social skills are more valued than their specific technical ability. To guard against inertia which could result from a lifetime attachment to one specific function, Japanese companies tend to move their employees around the organization, giving them new responsibilities in new areas. The system requires employees with adaptable attitudes.

The seniority system in Japanese firms is adopted from the Japanese family system, and takes the form of group employment, reassignment, and promotion at predictable and regular intervals.[12] Since hiring is done at regular intervals, there is a close relationship between an employee's age and the length of employment in the company. Promotions are based primarily on these two factors. However, realizing that an overly rigid system could lead to a total suppression of individual abilities, Japanese firms in recent years have started to reward more capable employees with bonuses and job assignments closer to key decision-making processes.

Coordination Strategy

In most U.S.-based MNCs, the function of each management position and the line of authority in the organization are clearly defined. In an individualistic society, such a clear delineation of responsibility is a prerequisite for the successful participation of each employee in the corporate setting. For U.S. business firms, an individual with a predetermined function is the basic unit of operation, and the systematic organization of such units drives the corporation toward its goals.[13]

However, this organization system puts an excessive premium on tangible short-term gains. Internal coordination of activities suffers from mechanistic relations among members of the organization. The focus on short-term results is an inherent part of the U.S. business environment, because managers are evaluated primarily by stockholders, who are mainly interested in achieving short-term capital gain.

Japanese companies, considering themselves assemblies of numerous sections, do not hire employees for specific functions or responsibilities.[14] Instead, employees are assigned to specific jobs after becoming members of a company. As corporate requirements change, employees are shifted around within the firm to meet particular needs; their workload and the nature of their work can vary considerably. Furthermore, the company demands collective responsibility of the smaller groups within the organization.

As previously noted, Japanese companies are driven by the desire for long-term accumulation of capital. The goal is pursued by having all members of the company, through their particular units, participate in the corporate decision-making process. Japanese companies generally maintain an excessive number of employees within the company. Compared to the U.S., the business environment in Japan tends to be less predictable, the labor force less mobile, and the capital market less developed. Therefore, Japanese companies can take advantage of unforeseen business opportunities only by maintaining a surplus of internal labor.

Such an organic organization has a tendency to meet all new challenges through adaptive responses only and is often unable to develop creative responses to new situations. When new business opportunities appear to be beyond the immediate grasp of their capabilities, Japanese firms often simply forego the opportunities. Similarly, rather than creatively responding to the challenge of overseas opportunities head-on through direct investment, Japanese companies tend to choose foreign trade as the adaptive response.

Financial Strategy

U.S.-based MNCs must rely on retained earnings or incur additional external debt to provide the capital for foreign direct investment. However, a company's financial soundness in the United States is often judged on the basis of its leverage ratio. Hence, the ability to undertake additional foreign direct investment is necessarily limited by the ability of U.S.-based MNCs to maintain an acceptable debt position. As a result, foreign direct investment occurs in stages and tends to be quite selective.

For the nine Japanese *sogo-shosha,* the average ratio of net equity to total assets was 3.9 percent in 1984. Such a high leverage ratio could not be sustained by a firm in the United States; such a firm would be regarded as insolvent. However, *sogo-shosha* enjoy the support of their business group and have direct access to a major group bank. The financial soundness of *sogo-shosha,* therefore, is a function of the strength of the groups they belong to.

Not only do *sogo-shosha* have almost limitless access to bank borrowings, they receive the lowest possible cost of fund. It is more difficult for smaller companies operating outside the large business groups to obtain external loans, and their cost of fund is generally 2-3 percent higher than that of *sogo-shosha.* Therefore, *sogo-shosha* often act as financial intermediaries, providing intercompany loans to smaller firms. Their purpose is not simply to make profits by charging a premium on these loans. Providing the loans gives the *sogo-shosha* an opportunity to gain the commercial right to supply raw materials and to distribute the products of the smaller companies.

Balance Between Line Functions

Throughout the history of U.S. corporations, the relationship between production managers and sales managers has been competitive. A typical U.S. business firm maintains two basic line functions of production and marketing, and a staff function that includes planning, finance, and personnel affairs. In any business firm, the value-added from production is realized only when a sale is completed. However, production coupled with extensive research and development capabilities drives the company toward new products and permits U.S.-based MNCs to maintain their technological edge in worldwide markets.

Japanese *sogo-shosha* do not possess any significant production capabilities and purposely rely on the products of other companies. *Sogo-shosha* base their operations on extensive information capabilities, deriving their value-added from their ability to match the buyer and the seller for any particular product.

Diversification Strategy

Most U.S. firms began as regional corporations, producing and marketing a single product to the immediate geographic area. After the 1880s, U.S. firms expanded through a series of intraindustry mergers. The rapid development of the U.S. transportation system, especially railroads, allowed regional companies to become national corporations. During the 1920s, a series of acquisitions of vertically related companies led larger firms to develop into integrated national corporations.

With increasing foreign direct investment after the 1920s, U.S.-based MNCs adopted a decentralized management structure, giving their overseas subsidiaries the responsibility for local operations. This geographic diversification demanded a wider perspective on business activities, and U.S. entrepreneurs sought to maximize the return on their overseas investment by engaging in functional activities such as transportation, warehousing, and financing, in addition to their traditional emphasis on production and marketing. The result was the emergence of multinational corporations.

The diversification strategy of these U.S.-based MNCs tended to be selective, based on the monopolistic advantage that they enjoyed in their established industry segments. Product diversification was generally limited to vertical integration into related industry segments, while area diversification was concentrated within certain regions, usually in other developed countries. Similarly, functional diversification was limited to activities that could immediately increase the profitability of the main line of manufacturing activities.

Among the three dimensions of diversification (product, area, and function), product is the least diversified by U.S.-based MNCs, except for certain conglomerates such as ITT. Traditional U.S.-based MNCs continue to specialize in a limited number of products based on extensive research and development. For example, General Motors continues to concentrate on automobile production, IBM on computers, and Exxon on oil and petrochemical products. Therefore, U.S.-based MNCs can be characterized as international business enterprises that have achieved selective diversification in geographic area and function, but which remain undiversified in product.

Japanese *sogo-shosha* began, in the late nineteenth century, as domestic trading companies intended to counter the increasing influence of foreign traders. After establishing their position in Japan's import market during the early twentieth century, Japanese trading companies sought export markets for their increasingly wide range of products. The result was the emergence prior to World War II of international trading companies, characterized by both market and product diversification.

After World War II, Japanese trading companies developed into marketing-oriented large trading companies. They began to establish foreign subsidiaries, and by the early 1960s formed an extensive international sales network with a direct presence in major foreign markets. These networks constituted a global logistics system which became the source of comparative advantage for Japan's large trading companies in international trade.[16]

In an attempt to discourage direct handling of overseas sales by Japanese manufacturers, Japanese trading companies sought to increase their activities beyond simple exports. The result was vertically oriented functional integration into numerous support activities, such as raw-material exploration and imports, transportation, and warehousing. In effect the traders became full-fledged diversified trading companies through functional integration.

A cursory comparison of the historical evolution of U.S.-based MNCs and Japanese *sogo-shosha* could lead to the impression that the two international business concerns have pursued a similar diversification strategy. However, there is a fundamental difference in the diversification strategies of the two. U.S.-based MNCs sought selective diversification. In contrast, Japanese *sogo-shosha* diversifed without restriction in product, area, or function as far as they could achieve economies of scale.

Business Strategies Summarized

Table 3-1 summarizes the differences in business strategies of U.S.-based MNCs and Japanese *sogo-shosha*. It is clear that U.S.-based MNCs and Japanese *sogo-shosha* are two distinct forms of international business organization and cannot be considered to be one form at different stages of maturity, as some scholars argue. The two forms are the products of the environments in their

Table 3-1
Business Strategies of U.S.-Based MNCs and Japanese *Sogo-Shosha*

	U.S.-Based MNCs	*Japanese Sogo-Shosha*
Internationalization	Foreign direct investment: export of factors of production and import of finished goods.	Foreign trade: import of raw materials and export of finished goods
External growth	Mergers and acquisitions	Formation of business groups
Organization	Decentralized by industry segments	Functional specialization and coordination
Personnel	Short-term employment and individual contract	Lifetime employment and seniority system
Coordination	Mechanistic and contractual	Organic and undefined
Finances	Internal funds and leveraging	Intermediation between banks and manufacturers
Line balance	Production *vs.* sales	Information and marketing
Diversification	Selective and based on monopolistic advantage	In all fronts to achieve economies of scale

respective countries. A unique set of political, economic, cultural, and social pressures formed the MNC in the United States and the GTC in Japan.

Therefore, neither the MNC form nor the GTC form can be easily offered as a corporate growth model for other countries. Different environmental pressures result in different business strategies for international companies. However, this does not mean that others cannot benefit from the experience of the United States or Japan. While each country will have to establish its own form of international business organization and choose appropriate strategies, each must understand how the strategies chosen by the U.S. MNCs and the Japanese *sogo-shosha* were groomed to their present forms.

Notes

1. Alfred D. Chandler, Jr., *The Visible Hand, The Managerial Revolution in American Business* (Cambridge, Mass.: Harvard University Press, 1977), chapter I.

2. Such a relocation of production sites can be explained by the product life cycle theory, originally stated by Raymond Vernon.

3. Kinichiro Toba, Yaku, *American Keieishi Jo, Ge* (Business History of America, Part 2) (Tokyo: Toyo Keizai Shimposha, 1977), 369.

4. Shijo Muramatsu, *Kigyo Gobenron* (Theory of Business Merger) (Tokyo: Dobunkan Shuppan Kabushiki Gaisha, 1973), 39-48.

5. Alexander K. Young, *Sogo Shosha: Japan's Multinational Trading Companies* (Boulder, Colo.: Westview Press, Inc., 1979) 83-117.

6. Shincho Tsuda, *Nihon Teki Keiei No Ronri* (The Logic of Japanese Management) (Tokyo: Chuo Keizaisha, 1978).

7. Gen Kubo, *Sogo Shosha To Sekaizaibatsu Gun* (Sogo Shosha and the World's Conglomerates) (Tokyo: Tokyo Nunoi Shuppan Kabushiki Gaisha, 1975), 35.

8. Alexander D. Chandler, Jr., *Strategy and Structure: Chapters in the History of the American Industrial Enterprise* (Cambridge, Mass.: The MIT Press, 1962), 78.

9. Shinichi Yonekawa, *Europe, America, Nihon No Keizai Hudo* (Business Climate of Europe, America and Japan) (Tokyo: Yuhikaku, 1978), 130.

10. Kinichiro Toba, Yaku, *American Keieishi Jo,* 243.

11. Mitsuo Fujii, Nado, *Keieishi-Nippon* (Business History of Japan) (Tokyo: Nihon Hyoronsha, 1982) 113-114.

12. Ryushi Itawa, *Nihon Teki Keiei No Hensei Genri* (The Principles of Japanese Management) (Tokyo: Bunchin Do, 1978), 215.

13. Ibid., 174-176.

14. Ibid., 169.

15. Dong-Sung Cho, *Kyungyoung Jeongchaek-kwa Changki Jeonryak Kyehoek* (Business Policy and Long-Range Strategic Planning) (Seoul: Youngji Moonhwasa, 1983), 227-228.

16. Kinugasa Yoho, *Nihon Kigyo No Kokusaika Senryaku* (The Internationalization Strategy of Japanese Firm) (Tokyo: Nihon Keizai Shimbunsha, 1979), 17-18.

4

The General Trading
Company Transplanted

During the 1970s, the consistent growth of Japanese *sogo-shosha* in the midst of the worldwide economic recession caught the eyes of policymakers in a number of countries. The governments of developing countries recognized *sogo-shosha* as a leading force in the Japanese export front and as a major cause of Japan's trade surplus. These countries started to develop their own GTC systems to survive the neoprotectionist moves adopted by major importing countries. Even the United States, whose keynote economic principle has been free enterprise with minimum government intervention beyond the regulation of monopolistic activities, enacted the Export Trading Company Act in October 1982 in the hopes of improving its deteriorating balance of trade.

This chapter first reviews the evolution of the Japanese *sogo-shosha* after World War II through a series of external challenges and internal responses. It then examines the establishment and growth of export-oriented trading companies in various countries since the 1970s and evaluates their performances. A key question is whether the GTC system that emerged in the distinctive Japanese environment can be successfully transplanted to another country. The development of GTCs in Korea provides a particularly useful test case. Similar developments in other countries, including Taiwan, Thailand, Turkey, and the United States, are also examined in order to judge the feasibility of applying the GTC model to different business environments.

Japanese *Sogo-Shosha*: A Prototype of the GTC

Today's *sogo-shosha* can be viewed as products of a series of adaptive responses to changes in the dynamics of their business environment. This section examines some of the major environmental pressures that pushed *sogo-shosha* into new strategic directions and continued growth since World War II. The Japanese experience can be divided into four separate stages: the period of growth in the early 1950s, the period of decline in the early 1960s, the period of criticism in the early 1970s, and the period of uncertainty in the early 1980s.

1950s: Period of Growth

The Korean War revealed Japanese trading companies' vulnerability to sudden changes in the external economic environment and confirmed the importance of wide-based internationalization for their future. When armistice negotiations seemed to spell an early end to the Korean War in March 1951, there was a sudden drop in the prices of three commodities—rubber, cotton, and fats—that *sogo-shosha* had been hoarding for future profits. Projecting future shortages, *sogo-shosha* had been importing raw materials at relatively high prices. The price decrease greatly reduced the profitability of *sogo-shosha;* indeed, some nearly became insolvent.

Continued stagnation in the trade sector forced the Japanese government to contemplate public support programs. The result was the implementation of various government subsidies for Japanese trading companies in 1953. New tax incentive programs included tax exemption on export income, tax credit on foreign investment, and accelerated depreciation on assets of foreign offices. Furthermore, to prevent overcompetition, the government allowed Japanese traders to coordinate their activities by establishing import associations and export agreements with each other.

Active government support programs helped *sogo-shosha* to rationalize their traditional operations and to increase their product range. In 1953, the Japanese government also instituted the export-import link system, which tied imports of specific lucrative products and raw materials to exports of specific heavy and chemical manufactures.[1] For example, import licenses for lucrative consumer goods such as bananas, whisky, and crude sugar were given to trading companies that had already met export targets for ships, machine tools, and other industrial goods. The exports of ships was particularly subsidized through the linking practice, for both shipbuilders and their export agent trading companies were allowed to split the profits from crude sugar imports. The policy effectively allowed export losses to be offset by import profits, thereby naturally encouraging trading companies to diversify their products.

The holding companies of Mitsubishi and Mitsui, which were dissolved in 1946, were gradually reunited in 1954 and 1959, respectively, to form even more powerful companies. During the vacancy of these two powerhouses, however, the textile traders of Kansai areas diversified to become the sizable *sogo-shosha* of C. Itoh & Co., the Marubeni Corporation, Toyo Menka Kaisha, Kanematsu Gosho, and Nichimen Company, while the metal traders of Nissho-Iwai Co. and Ataka & Co. also formed *sogo-shosha.*[2] From the ashes of the holding company of Suimitomo Zaibatsu, which was also dissolved in 1946, Sumitomo Shoji emerged as a formidable member of the trading community by the early 1950s.[3]

1960s: Period of Decline

By the early 1960s, many observers of the Japanese economy were predicting a permanent decline in the role of *sogo-shosha,* for two major reasons. First, there was a significant increase in the direct participation of Japanese manufacturing firms in both export and import markets. As a result of the rapid economic growth during the 1950s, Japanese manufacturers reached a scale where they could afford to establish their own independent trade networks. *Sogo-shosha* were able to maintain their share in the trade of low value-added products such as steel and shipbuilding; however, their role as exporters of high value-added products, such as automobiles and televisions, began an irreversible decline. Second, diseconomies of scale resulted from continued product diversification, which led to an increasingly complex organizational structure and relative increase in operating expense. To avert the possibility of permanent decline, the *sogo-shosha* searched for new avenues of growth. The activities of Mitsui and Mitsubishi are examples of increased functional diversification.

As a sales and purchasing agent for a cohesive group of giant industrial and service companies that are particularly strong in chemical and heavy industrial sectors, Mitsubishi grew rapidly. Since its reunification in 1954, Mitsubishi has not lost the number one position among the *sogo-shosha* except a few years (1959, 1965, and 1966) to Mitsui. Its early participation in oil import business led the company into the LNG project in Alaska in 1960, and a few years later in Brunei, which became the single most important source of income in the late 1970s.[4]

Mitsui's reunification did not proceed as smoothly and swiftly as that of Mitsubishi. Even by 1959, Mitsui could not regroup all its former businesses. The defection of General Bussan, for example, played a critical role in Mitsui's failure to catch up with Mitsubishi. General Bussan had taken over Mitsui's oil trade contracts, leaving Mitsui to start over in building up oil business. Based on relatively limited business areas, Mitsui began to pursue vertical integration aggressively. For example, it integrated backward into poultry and hog farming, and forward into supermarkets, shopping centers, and chain stores. The result was a rapid entrance into the Japanese mass consumer market. Mitsui also diversified into new ventures including plant and project exports, which eventually brought the company to its disastrous petrochemical project in Iran.

1970s: Period of Criticism

Sogo-shosha established themselves as fully diversified GTCs in the 1960s by successfully meeting the challenge from Japanese manufacturers and overcoming weaknesses in their own internal operations. Entering the 1970s, however, *sogo-shosha* were again confronted with dynamic changes in the business environment. First, there was a slowdown in the growth of the

Japanese economy, particularly in the steel, shipbuilding, and petrochemical industries. Second, there was a shift in the economic and industrial structure of Japan, with the economic course increasingly dictated by consumers rather than manufacturers. Third, after the Nixon declaration in 1971, the fluctuation in currency values made export performance less predictable. Fourth, the oil crisis was particularly hard-felt in Japan, which is almost totally dependent on foreign energy imports. Finally, increased competition for market share and speculative activities among *sogo-shosha* fueled the inflation in Japan.

As a mood of uncertainty spread throughout the economy, prominent *sogo-shosha* became the subject of growing public criticism due to their speculation and profiteering in the areas of stocks and land and commodities such as wool, yarn, soybeans, and wood. Most of these practices were not illegal and were justified by *sogo-shosha* on the grounds that land was needed for construction of buildings and houses, that stockholding was one of the functions of *sogo-shosha,* and that commodities were bought abroad. Nevertheless, the huge profits scored by *sogo-shosha* in the midst of high inflation and economic recession in the mid 1970s brought the Fair Trade Commission and then the government into the scene.

Some of the criticisms other than speculative behaviors against Japanese *sogo-shosha* are summarized here:

Issue	Criticism
Size	Too large for the size of the national economy
Financing	Collusion with banks, priority in trade financing
Market behavior	Hoarding and cornering the market, speculative activities, evasion of law, collaboration with politicians, monopoly over market information
Organization	Increasing trend toward rigid and inhuman management structure
Market domination	Through acquisition of small and medium-sized companies
Business groups	Increasing concentration of capital leading to reemergence of *zaibatsu*

Concerned with increasing public criticism and mounting pressure from the government, the Japanese Traders Association, which often acts as the united front for *sogo-shosha,* proclaimed new standards of behavior in future *sogo-shosha* operations. These included:

1. *Sogo-shosha* will not make speculative investment in real estate, securities, or essential commodities;

2. *Sogo-shosha* will make an effort to contribute to the increased welfare of ordinary consumers;

3. *Sogo-shosha* will give due consideration to the effects of any new project development on the local environment and the concerns of local inhabitants; and

4. In case of an acquisition, *sogo-shosha* will consider the interest and concerns of the acquired company.

In following these standards, Mitsui allocated 2-4 percent of its profits before tax to antipollution programs and other social services. Mitsubishi redefined internal standards of operations, reassigning product and functional responsibilities among the various business units in order to be responsible to the needs of the employees and the society. Mitsubishi's apparent willingness to cater to social needs came to be expressed in the sentiment that "Mitsubishi's profit is Japan's profit." As a result of this responsiveness by management, *sogo-shosha* continued to grow in size and play an important role in the Japanese economy. In 1979, nine *sogo-shosha* together handled 48.2 percent of the nation's total exports and 54.5 percent of imports, as shown in table 4-1.

1980s: Period of Uncertainty

Close cooperation between the government and the business sector in the aftermath of the oil crisis allowed Japan to become the leading player in the international trade arena by the late 1970s. However, Japan's nationalistic economic policies antagonized other countries, and with the European economy still relatively stagnant, and the United States, particularly its automobile industry, increasingly critical, Japan's unrelenting policy of importing raw materials and exporting high value-added finished goods became untenable.

Table 4-1
***Sogo-Shosha*'s Share in the Japanese Economy**
(billions of yen)

	1969	*1974*	*1979*	*1984*
Japan				
GNP (A)	64,520.8	139,256.5	224,866.3	292,796.0
Exports (B)	6,047.2	17,079.6	24,479.6	40,325.3
Imports (C)	5,761.2	18,276.2	27,601.8	32,321.1
C/B	0.95	1.07	1.13	0.80
Nine *Sogo-Shosha*				
Total Revenues (D)	16,599.0	46,872.3	61,734.1	84,051.6
Exports (E)	2,339.5	9,577.8	11,798.4	16,806.9
Imports (F)	3,586.5	10,465.4	15,054.8	19,846.3
Share				
D/A	25.7	33.7	27.5	28.7
E/B	38.7	56.1	48.2	41.7
F/C	62.3	57.3	54.5	61.4

Source: Yamaichi Research Institute, *Industrial Statistics*, 1984.

At the same time, small and medium-sized companies in Japan started gaining direct access to financial institutions, effectively decimating the traditional role of *sogo-shosha* as financial intermediaries between banks and manufacturers.

Further, there was a fundamental change in Japan's industrial structure. The industries based on imported raw materials, such as petrochemicals, steel, and machinery, were rapidly being replaced by technology-intensive industries, such as semiconductors, robotics, and electronics. As a result, the ratio of imports to exports decreased continuously from 1.13 in 1979 to 0.80 in 1984, as shown in table 4-1. This change reflects a continued decrease in raw material imports, eroding one of the mainstays of *sogo-shosha*'s operations. Although the contributions of nine *sogo-shosha* to Japan's imports reached 61.4 percent in 1984, this indicates the vulnerability that *sogo-shosha* face in the declining import market.

The financial performances of *sogo-shosha* were also dissatisfactory, with an average return on sales and equity ratio standing at 0.07 percent and 4.4 percent, respectively, in 1984, as shown in table 4-2. For the *sogo-shosha,* the early 1980s were a period of uncertainty.[5]

Faced with stagnation in their traditional activities, *sogo-shosha* are again at a crossroad. Many, if not all, are changing their strategic directions by emphasizing third-country trade, pursuing foreign direct investment, increasing investment in research and development, expanding energy-related business, and adopting a long-term management plan. Increasing third-country trade should not present a problem, since it falls well within the *sogo-shosha*'s traditional international trade capabilities. As table 4-3 shows, the share of third-country trade ranges from 11.3 percent to 31.8 percent among nine

Table 4-2
Financial Performance of Japanese *Sogo-Shosha*, April 1983-March 1984
(billions of yen)

Sogo-Shosha	Sales	Net Profit	Return on Sales (%)[a]	Total Assets	Stockholders' Equity	Equity Ratio (%)
Mitsubishi	15,029	20.3	0.14	5,164	309	6.0
Mitsui	13,960	6.2	0.04	4,500	199	4.4
C. Itoh	12,987	3.4	0.03	3,388	90	2.6
Marubeni	11,821	3.7	0.03	3,597	120	3.3
Sumitomo	11,624	18.7	0.16	2,152	178	8.3
Nissho-Iwai	7,790	5.8	0.07	2,386	91	3.8
Toya-Menka	4,053	2.2	0.05	1,411	47	3.3
Kanematsu-Gosho	3,489	0.1	0.002	1,083	25	2.3
Nichimen	3,298	1.5	0.05	1,155	32	2.8
Total	84,051	61.9	—	24,836	1,091	—
Average	9,339	6.9	0.07	2,760	121	4.4

[a]Return on sales is calculated as net profit divided by sales.

[b]Equity ratio is calculated as stockholders' equity divided by total assets.

Table 4-3

Trade Activities of Japanese *Sogo-Shosha*, April 1983-March 1984

Sogo-Shosha	Exports (%)	Imports (%)	Third-Country Trade (%)	Domestic Commerce (%)	Total (billions of yen)
Mitsubishi	17.7	34.3	11.7	36.3	15,029.2
Mitsui	17.8	27.1	16.0	39.1	13,960.4
C. Itoh	16.8	19.4	17.7	46.1	12,987.3
Marubeni	28.4	19.8	16.9	34.9	11,820.9
Sumitomo	22.6	15.2	11.3	50.9	11,624.3
Nisho-Iwai	16.8	26.7	21.1	35.4	7,789.8
Toyo-Menka	23.1	23.1	16.8	37.0	4,053.2
Kanematsu-Gosho	14.4	21.6	15.0	49.0	3,489.0
Nichimen	22.8	15.6	31.8	29.8	3,297.5
Total					84,051.6

Source: Yamaichi Research Institute, *Industrial Statistics*, 1981.

sogo-shosha, and this share has steadily risen over the years. It remains to be seen, however, whether their efforts in the four relatively new activities will prove successful.

Scholars and practitioners frequently note that Japanese businessmen tend to be ethnocentric, an orientation not conducive to foreign direct investment, which demands the export of indigenous capital resources.[6] Foreign direct investment further requires the willingness to reinvest in local operations without repatriation of earnings in the early stages of the operation. It is not at all certain that Japanese businessmen will be able to successfully manage new challenges offered by foreign direct investment. Therefore, it appears that *sogo-shosha* will continue to concentrate on related foreign direct investments to support their ongoing operations. For example, Mitsubishi's recent investment in an Indonesian plywood company constituted a backward integration from its acquisition of an interior decorating company in California. Similarly, as a forward integration from its poultry broiler and feed operations, Mitsubishi invested in Kentucky Fried Chicken stores.

Investment in research and development may prove to be the most difficult activity for the *sogo-shosha.* Their current financial resources do not permit a significant increase in research and development expenditures. Further, they do not have their own manufacturing capabilities to take advantage of any technological breakthroughs. Therefore, the most predictable course for *sogo-shosha* is to become traders of technology. In the past, *sogo-shosha* organized the transfer of foreign technology into Japan by establishing joint ventures between domestic manufacturers and technology-rich foreign investors. In the future, *sogo-shosha* can be expected to pursue transfer of technology systematically as a profit-making operation.

The success of Mitsubishi in its joint venture with Royal Dutch Shell in a liquified natural gas operation in Brunei spurred other *sogo-shosha* into energy business expansion programs. After investment, profits from the Brunei operations accounted for one-third of Mitsubishi's total profits. Other *sogo-shosha,* however, have been less successful. The ill-fated investment by Ataka in an oil refinery in Nova Scotia culminated in Ataka's insolvency. Mitsui's participation in the Iran-Japan Petrochemical Complex ended in huge losses. It is not certain that other *sogo-shosha* have the ability to successfully increase their investment in energy-related industries.

Sogo-shosha have adopted a long-term management planning policy to rationalize the structure of their diversified operations. By reexamining the future of their numerous operations, they should be able to streamline their operations, concentrating in their areas of strength. However, their bottom-up, collective decision-making process may prove inimical to rapid changes. The initial focus will be the issue of profitability, which has long been a secondary concern to *sogo-shosha.*

The five strategies we have discussed are shared by the *sogo-shosha* today, but none of these strategies seem to offer a clear path out of the present uncertainty over future growth. Nevertheless, the ability of *sogo-shosha* to adapt to new environmental pressures has contributed to their persistent growth in times of both economic recession and expansion in the past. *Sogo-shosha* will continue to play an important role within the Japanese economy no matter what paths they choose for the future.

Korean GTCs

Korea's GTCs had existed for only 10 years as of 1985. Their rapid growth during this period, however, made them a visible force in international trade. Some Korean GTCs export more than $3 billion. Their contribution to the national economy is comparable to that of Japanese *sogo-shosha,* in that their combined exports are close to 50 percent of the national total. Given this impressive record, Korean GTCs are widely recognized as being one of the most successful adopters of the Japanese GTC model. In the course of such rapid growth, however, a number of undesirable side effects have caused the deterioration of their profitability.[7]

Background

The Korean economy has grown rapidly since the early 1960s with the implementation of a series of five-year economic plans. The government adopted the strategy of using exports to fuel the rapid economic growth. As a result, Korea's exports, which amounted to a mere $30 million in 1962, reached $100 million in 1964, $1 billion in 1971, $10 billion in 1977, and $30 billion by 1985.

This geometric expansion of exports was made possible by various government subsidies to exporters through financing, tax exemption, and manipulation of foreign exchange rates. As export growth continued, however, these support programs became too costly for the government to maintain. Furthermore, they resulted in various undesirable side effects such as the proliferation of small-scale manufacturer-exporters, overcompetition between exporters in overseas markets, and the overdependence of exporters on the government. In addition, the need for Korean exporters to aggressively penetrate new overseas markets became a pressing issue as worldwide recession and protective trade policies among developed countries emerged after the oil crisis in 1973.

The political situation of the ruling party in Korea was also in a critical phase in the early 1970s. In 1972, President Park Chung-Hee initiated a constitutional amendment that gave him an unlimited tenure. In order to justify his prolonged leadership, Park presented a blueprint for continued economic growth, summed up in slogans such as "per capita GNP $1,000," "$10 billion exports," and "my-car age," to be reached by 1978. The actual export volume in 1974, however, fell short of the target set earlier in that year, and the government became desperate to bridge the gap between political goals and economic performance. It was at this time that the resilience of the Japanese economy, supported in part by the *sogo-shosha,* attracted policymakers in Korea.

Faced with a slowdown in economic growth, the government policymakers conceived an idea of developing general trading companies, organizations large enough to attain economies of scale in the world market, specialized enough in exports to gain international competitiveness, self-sufficient and independent from government support, and capable of systematic overseas marketing. They also expected that a few GTCs, which together would handle about half of Korea's exports, would be much easier to control than thousands of small exporters. In short, the GTC system institutionalized export activities in Korea.

Requisites for Korean GTC Designation

In April 1975, the Ministry of Commerce and Industry announced an ordinance specifying the minimum requisites for receiving a GTC designation. These were:

1. Paid-in-capital of one billion won (approximately $2.5 million)
2. Annual exports of $50 million
3. Seven products with an export value in excess of $500 thousand each
4. Ten overseas branch offices
5. Ten countries with an export value of over $1 million each
6. Public offering of GTC stocks

These requisites reflected the policymakers' conception of the GTC. First, although named GTC, a firm was not expected to be more than a general export company. Second, the minimum capital requirement of one billion won and annual exports of $50 million destined the GTC to be a large-scale trader. Third, the minimum requirement of seven products mandated that the GTC diversify its exports. Fourth, the requirement for minimum number of branch offices and ten countries with an export value in excess of $1 million each demanded that the GTC diversify export markets. Fifth, public stock offering provided the GTC with a mechanism to generate additional capital from the market but at the same time put pressure on managers to maintain satisfactory stock prices, which in turn compelled them to pay substantial dividends from the founding of the company. Sixth, there was no requirement to promote the GTC's functional diversification, such as in financing, insurance, or transportation. This last point marks a sharp difference between Korean GTCs and their Japanese counterparts.

The ordinance governing the Korean GTC system underwent a series of amendments as the economic environment and government policies changed during the 1975-81 period. While there was little change in the subsidy program, the requisites for GTC designation were revised six times. As shown in table 4-4, the export value requisites were periodically adjusted to accommodate the government's continuing emphasis on export expansion. The minimum export value went from $50 million in 1975 to $100 million in 1976, $150 million in 1977, and to 2 percent of total Korean exports in 1978 through 1985.

On the other hand, policymakers decreased requirements that the GTCs further diversify their products and markets. Since 1978, the minimum requirement for number of export countries and export share to selected areas in the Middle East, Africa, and Latin America have been dropped. Furthermore, the minimum number of export items was reduced from ten to five. In 1981, all requisites were deleted except the minimum export value and public offering of stocks. Given these drastic changes, it appears that the GTC system as a government institution no longer exists.

Designation of Korean GTCs

The government designated Samsung Trading Company as the first Korean GTC on May 19, 1975, followed by Ssangyong, Daewoo, Kukje, and Hanil during the same year. In 1976, six more companies were designated GTCs: Koryo, Hyosung, Bando, Sunkyong, Samwha, and Kumho. In 1978, Yulsan and Hyundai were added for a total of thirteen Korean GTCs.

The Yulsan Group, which was once envied for its sales growth from a mere $4.8 million in 1975 to over $187 million in 1978, went bankrupt in

Table 4-4
Change of Requisites for Korean GTCs

	1975	1976	1977	1978	1979	1980	1981	1985
Requisites for Designation								
Minimum annual export	$50 m	$100 m	$150 m	2% of total export	2% of total export	2% of total export	2% of total export	2% of total export
Minimum capital	W1 b	W1.5 b	W2 b	—	—	—	—	—
Export items over $1 m	7[a]	10	10	5	5	5	—	—
Export countries over $1 m	10	15	20	—	—	—	—	—
Number of overseas branch offices	10	15	20	20	20	20	—	—
Public offering of stocks			Mandatory	Mandatory	Mandatory	Mandatory	Mandatory	Mandatory
Export to special areas			b					
Discretionary power of government							Explicitly reserved	Explicitly reserved
Number of GTCs	5	11	11	13	12	10	10	9
Emphasis	Export promotion	Penetration into frontier regions	Limit in the number of GTC to 10	Drastic relaxation of requisites			Deemphasizing GTC	
Cause for Change	Crisis in export growth	Diplomatic motive (vote at UN)	$10 b export achieved	GTCs' bargaining power increased			Controversy over GTCs' performance	Psychological and institutional merits of GTCs disappeared

[a]More than $500,000.
[b]Middle East, 15%; Latin America, 3%; Africa, 3%; branch offices, two in each region above.

early 1979, resulting in the liquidation of Yulsan Trading Company. In 1980, Hanil and Samwha failed to retain GTC status, as their respective exports in 1979 of $237 million and $195 million fell short of the critical $301 million mark, which represented 2 percent of Korean total for the year. Kumho failed to reach the 2 percent mark in 1983, losing the title in 1984. The requisites did not apply to Koryo, which was established and managed by the government for the purpose of fostering export activities of small- and medium-sized manufacturers. Therefore, nine Korean GTCs remained at the beginning of 1985.

Government Subsidies for Korean GTCs

To promote the export performance of Korean GTCs, the Ministry of Commerce and Industry offered the following subsidies:

Trade Administration

1. Priority to international traders of over $500 thousand offered by government agencies
2. Relaxation of the requirements for joining various commodity export associations
3. Right to import major raw materials for Korean GTC's own use

Financing

1. Export financing
2. Inventory financing for finished goods
3. Import financing for raw materials

Foreign Exchange Administration

1. The use of revolving letters of credit
2. Special treatment in controlling overseas branches
3. Increase in the limit of foreign currency holding by overseas branches

Most of these subsidies were subsequently made available to other large-scale exporters, after their incessant complaints. As a result, Korean GTCs did not consider government subsidies to be a big help to their businesses. Korean businessmen, nevertheless, were eager to have their companies designated as GTCs because, first, the GTC title could enhance a company's credibility, both in Korea and in foreign markets; second, it could help a company obtain concessions on various government-initiated projects, such as heavy industry and chemical plants; and third, owning a GTC could give the owner-manager a great sense of accomplishment as an entrepreneur.

Table 4-5
Exports of Korean GTCs
(millions of dollars)

GTC	1975	1976	1977	1978	1979	1980	1981	1982	1983
Samsung	223	335	507	493	769	1,237	1,620	1,860	2,225
Ssangyong	125	141	176	264	425	650	756	971	1,035
Daewoo	161	301	501	706	1,119	1,415	1,914	1,971	2,493
Kukje	64	197	328	472	564	742	849	934	861
Hyosung	34	113	199	338	585	761	787	599	687
Bando	31	134	212	330	471	493	619	689	1,065
Sunkyong	56	114	247	283	334	431	585	601	661
Kumho	32	99	204	256	305	357	190	166	178
Hyundai	–	–	320	260	615	1,028	1,723	2,667	3,133
Koryo	12	18	24	31	51	67	84	75	80
Korean Exports	5,427	8,115	10,474	12,713	15,055	17,055	20,993	21,616	24,222
GTC Exports	739	1,476	2,884	3,584	5,238	7,183	9,127	10,535	12,418
GTC Exports as % of Korean Exports	13.6	18.2	27.5	28.2	34.8	41.0	43.5	48.1	51.3

Performance of Korean GTCs

Exports. Table 4-5 shows the historical performance of Korean GTCs in terms of export amount. Hyundai ranked first in 1983, with exports of $3,133 million, 27.4 percent of the total Korean GTCs' exports for the year. Daewoo and Samsung followed Hyundai, with $2,493 million and $2,225 million, respectively, while the remaining GTCs achieved exports between $80 million and $1,065 million. Altogether, the ten GTCs exported $10,535 million in 1982 and $12,418 million in 1983, equivalent to 48.1 percent and 51.3 percent, respectively, of total Korean exports.

Among the items exported by Korean GTCs, heavy industrial goods increased most rapidly, with their share of the total exports rising from 47.7 percent in 1977 to 54.9 percent in 1980 and to 66.0 percent in 1983. The 1983 figure compared favorably with the Korean average of 55.7 percent.

However, Korean GTCs' dependence on the traditional export markets in North America, Western Europe, Japan, and Asia stayed unchanged, accounting for 75.0 percent of their total exports in 1983 compared to 79.3 percent in 1977. Relatively new markets in the Middle East, Latin America, Oceania, and Africa accounted for 25.0 percent of exports by GTCs in 1983; this figure was not very different from the 23.6 percent share for Korean exports as a whole.

Imports. In 1983, Korean GTCs as a group imported $2,166 million worth of goods, which constituted only 8.3 percent of the national total. Compared with the 55 to 65 percent of the total Japanese imports that Japanese *sogoshosha* have traditionally contributed, Korean GTCs' role in importation has been insignificant.

Finances. In spite of their contribution to the quantitative expansion of Korean exports, Korean GTCs' equity positions have deteriorated, and their profitabilities have nosedived over the years (see table 4-6). The major causes of this financial erosion are presented schematically in figure 4-1. Some of these factors must be examined in more detail for us to understand the causes of Korean GTCs' deteriorating financial performance.

Big Initial Investment and Long Pay-Back Period. A GTC must operate a certain number of overseas offices, which directly deal with local marketing, financing, and information gathering. Korean GTCs maintain eighteen to sixty foreign offices, each of which requires annual expenditures from a few hundred thousand to several million dollars. Most of these expenditures are for positioning the offices firmly within local markets rather than for generating short-term profits and therefore should be treated as investments. However, neither accounting principles nor management attitudes accept such

Table 4-6
Financial Position of Korean GTCs
(percent)

GTC	Return on Sales			Equity/Asset Ratio		
	1977	*1980*	*1983*	*1977*	*1980*	*1983*
Samsung	0.5	0.3	0.4	12.0	14.1	16.7
Ssangyong	1.0	0.3	0.1	8.9	7.6	6.2
Daewoo	5.0	1.8	1.1	25.7	20.6	17.4
Kukje	2.4	0.4	0.3	26.2	11.1	11.8
Hyosung	0.9	0	0.1	13.9	5.9	14.3
Bando	0.4	0.1	0.3	12.5	13.2	13.2
Sunkyong	0.8	0.3	0.3	9.7	6.2	7.8
Kumho	1.3	0.4	0.4	14.2	7.1	
Hyundai	0.3	0.3	0.3	48.4	5.4	17.4
Average	1.4	0.4	0.3	18.8	10.1	14.2

intangible expenditures as investment. As a result, these expenditures have been treated as expenses, laying a heavy burden on Korean GTCs' profit and loss statements.

Government's Emphasis on Export Amount. The government's primary objective in establishing Korean GTCs was to promote exports, and it has used all sorts of means to increase the exports of Korean GTCs. As a stick, the government annually increased the minimum requisite export amount that a Korean GTC must reach to retain its GTC title. As a carrot, the government created a variety of prizes, citations, and medals. More important, it provided low-cost financing for each dollar exported, which often more than compensated for losses incurred in export transactions. These government measures, together with the competitive spirit of the management, encouraged Korean GTCs to vie fiercely against each other to increase the export amount. In certain years, overenthusiastic competition resulted in malpractices such as export account purchasing, buying the title of export sales from a Korean manufacturer at a price 2-4 cents per dollar above the export value that was transferred directly between manufacturers and overseas buyers. Such behavior resulted in further deterioration in the profitability of Korean GTCs.

Increase in Interest Rates and Foreign Exchange Losses. Starting in late 1978, the U.S. prime rate moved up from less than 10 percent to more than 15 percent within a year. Korean GTCs, which had relied on foreign financing as a source of their long-term capital, were hard hit by this increase. Furthermore, the Korean government changed its foreign exchange system from a fixed to a floating one in January 1980, concurrently with a major devaluation from 485 to 580 wons per U.S. dollar, and in 1985 to 830 wons per dollar.

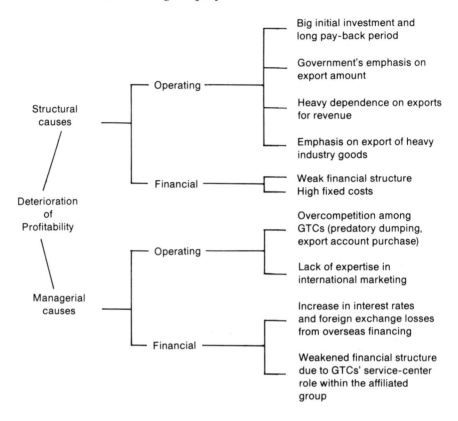

Figure 4-1. Causes of Korean GTCs' Deteriorating Financial Performance

These changes resulted in a heavy burden as Korean GTCs tried to pay off their long-term loans to foreign lenders.

Future of Korean GTCs

In January 1981, the government deleted all but two requisites for Korean GTCs, continuing to promote exports while freeing the GTCs from a prescribed mold. In effect, the Korean GTC system was transformed to a large trading company system, and GTCs are now at a crossroad. In the past, they simply pursued the path directed by the government, their only choice being to move either rapidly or slowly. Now they face several strategic choices, and it remains to be seen whether their managers can establish long-term objectives and successfully implement policies for continued growth.

Taiwanese LTCs

The Taiwanese government made a relatively early effort to promote exports by setting up a company to engage specifically in trade-related businesses. In 1966, Taiwan established China Trade and Development Corporation, with 40-percent government ownership, to administer warehousing, freight, and trade. In 1972, a group of independent Taiwanese businessmen established Transworld Trading Company to facilitate the exports of small- and medium-sized manufacturers. However, lack of experience and expertise, and eventually the oil crisis, led to the liquidation of both companies in 1973.

The economic health of Taiwan, always heavily dependent on the strength of exports, began to suffer during the worldwide recession following the oil crisis. With their own exports relatively stagnant, policymakers in Taiwan noticed the apparent success of Korean GTCs in promoting exports. The Taiwanese government reexamined the concept of export-oriented trading companies and sought to establish its own GTC system in the late 1970s.

At the same time, the government saw an opportunity to reduce Taiwan's dependence on foreign traders through the GTC system. In 1978, Japanese and American companies accounted for 65 percent of Taiwan's total trade volume, and 60 to 70 percent of exports by small- and medium-sized manufacturers. By delegating export responsibilities to Taiwan's trading companies, the government hoped that local manufacturing firms would also benefit from increased productivity resulting from functional specialization.

Requisites for Taiwanese LTC Designation

In November 1977, the Taiwanese government announced an ordinance outlining the minimum requisites for establishing a *large trading company*. These were:

1. Paid-in-capital of NT$200 million (approximately $5.6 million)
2. Incorporation for at least one year, with exports of $10 million during the year prior to LTC designation
3. Three overseas branch offices

In addition, the government demanded that 10 percent of outstanding shares of each LTC be held by a commercial bank.

LTCs operating strictly as export agents for Taiwanese manufacturing firms had a minimum annual export requirement of $20 million. Such LTCs, however, were not required to have overseas branch offices at the time of LTC designation, provided they set up three branches within one year.

Designation of Taiwanese GTCs

After moving to Taiwan in 1949, Chiang Kai-Shek's Kuomintang government made equal income distribution a stated part of its economic goal. To maintain this basic tenet of economic policy, the government sought both to avoid concentration of wealth by creating LTCs as entities independent of existing enterprise groups, and to prevent overcompetition among Taiwanese exporters. The government, therefore, created large trading companies through mergers or joint ventures between commercial banks, existing small trading companies, and small- and medium-sized manufacturers.

In September 1978, the government designated Pan Overseas Corporation as the first LTC. Four other companies—Collins Company, Nanlien International (or Taiwan United International Corp.), Great International, and E-Hsin International—followed. Background information on these five LTCs is summarized in table 4-7.

Government Subsidies for Taiwanese LTCs

According to the 1977 ordinance providing guidelines for establishing LTCs, and the 1980 ordinance promoting their export activities, the following subsidies were granted to LTCs:

1. Preferential treatment in financing based on a letter of credit. In some cases financing without mortgage was allowed.
2. Maximum of 25 percent on taxable income as corporate income tax and value-added tax.
3. Bonded processing allowed.
4. The right to provide import financing guarantee to small- and medium-sized companies.
5. Self-settlement of accounts allowed for importing raw materials used in export products.

Most of these benefits, however, have also been granted to manufacturers of export products, except for the right to guarantee import financing for small- and medium- sized companies.

Performance of Taiwanese GTCs

As shown in table 4-8, the aggregate exports of the five Taiwanese LTCs in 1981 and 1982 were limited to $235 million and $265 million, respectively, or about 1 percent of the national totals in those years. In the list of major Taiwanese exporters for 1981, Collins ranked nineteenth, E-Hsin International twentieth,

Table 4-7
Profiles of Taiwanese LTCs, End of 1983

	Date of Establishment or Designation	Capital (NT$ million)	Total Employees	Establishing Group	Overseas Offices	Major Product Segments	Major Markets
Pan Overseas Corp.	1978	215	127	14 overseas Chinese-owned Companies based in Southeast Asia; 6 local trading companies; 20 local manufacturers	6	Textiles, Electronics	North America Southeast Asia Mideast (70%)
Collins Co.	1979	200	203	13 year-old Collins Trading Co. designated as a LTC	5	Clothing, plastic goods, wooden products, other general merchandise	North America (90%)
Nanlien International	1979	800	67	Tainan Textile Group Companies; 40 local trading companies; China Int'l Commerce Bank	5	Food, textile, iron and steel, cement	USA, Japan Mideast, Hongkong
Great International	1979	600	126	Wechuan Foods Group Companies (35% of ownership); China Farmers Bank (15%); others	4	Frozen and canned food, machinery	USA Japan (70%)
E-Hsin International	1980	400 (paid-in-capital of 230)	106	3 banks and local trading companies	3	Textiles, electronics, metals	North America, Southeast Asia, Mideast (75%)

Sources: *Daily Economic Newspaper* October 25, 1982; *Business Asia* November 17, 1978, and September 24, 1982; *Industrial Newsletter* 13 (8, 1983): 31.

Table 4-8
Exports of Taiwanese LTCs
(millions of dollars)

LTC	1979	1980	1981	1982	1983[a]
Pan Overseas	19.1	37.3	42.2	42.2	17.9
Collins Company	32.2	57.9	69.1	73.6	58.3
Nanlien International	1.5	15.6	32.2	20.2	2.4
Great International	0.7	15.1	23.7	25.1	1.4
E-Hsin International	[b]	35.8	67.4	104.1	51.7
Total	53.5	161.7	234.6	265.2	131.8
Share of Taiwan's total (%)		0.82	1.04	1.19	1.15

Sources: *Business Asia* September 7, 1982; *Industrial Newsletter* 13 (8, 1983): 33.
[a]First six months of 1983.
[b]E-Hsin International was not designated as a LTC in 1979.

Pan Overseas twenty-eighth, Nanlien International forty-eighth, and Great International fiftieth.

These figures vividly show that Taiwanese LTCs did not have the same immediate impact on exports as Korean GTCs. In September 1982, about 55 percent of total Taiwanese exports were handled by Japanese *sogo-shosha*; American and European MNCs accounted for another 10 percent, leaving the remaining 35 percent for indigenous companies. A few local trade associations accounted for 10 percent of the national total, while about 15,000 Taiwanese manufacturing firms handled directly another 10 percent. As a result, over 30,000 Taiwanese trading companies and traders were left to compete for 15 percent of total Taiwanese exports. Because of this over-competition, only one LTC, Collins Company, was able to report profitable results for 1981.

In 1982, the newcomer E-Hsin International moved to the top, exporting over $100 million. On the other hand, Nanlien's exports were reduced drastically, while the other three LTCs stayed at about the same level. In the first six months of 1983, Great International and Nanlien collapsed to almost zero level.

A few factors explain the relatively lackluster performance of the LTCs. With a minimum paid-in-capital requirement of only NT$200 million each, Taiwanese LTCs were insufficiently capitalized. Furthermore, Taiwanese LTCs did not have the implicit support of established enterprise groups, giving them a limited debt capacity to finance working-capital requirements, and an inability to establish an extensive overseas marketing network. Trade associations continued to monopolize exports of profitable goods such as canned pine-apples, asparagus, and metal products, while publicly managed companies continued to trade independently. Anxious to retain their export licenses by meeting the minimum export requirement of $200 thousand, even small- and medium-sized manufacturers continued to export independently. As a result, LTCs found themselves exporting general merchandise with low profit margins.[8] In addition, due to the policymakers' unwillingness to give the LTCs a more prominent place in Taiwan's export efforts, there was a general lack of awareness of the role of the LTCs, and the LTCs suffered from the same inability as other Taiwanese companies to retain trained staff, who often left for better pay or to set up their own trading companies.

In December 1982, the ordinance specifying the minimum requisites for receiving the LTC designation was amended. This reflected the government's increasing emphasis on export amount. The LTC designation now required a company to export $20 million in 1982, up from $10 million in the 1977 ordinance. The subsequent required amounts were exports of $30 million in 1983 for a 1984 LTC title, $50 million in 1984 for 1985 title, and $100 million in 1985 for a 1986 LTC title, with future export requirements to be announced at a later date. There were little or no changes in the requisites on establishment of overseas branch offices or paid-in-capital.

Because Taiwanese LTCs have yet to contribute significantly to a quantitative expansion of exports, any special treatment for the LTCs could result in public criticism. Therefore it is not surprising that policymakers chose not to extend new subsidies in the recent amendment. Without a more active government support program, it remains to be seen whether the LTCs will be able to reduce Taiwan's dependence on foreign companies in international trade, or whether they will simply continue to coexist with the Japanese *sogo-shosha* as another outlet for Taiwan exports.

Thailand's ITCs

Although Thailand had a chronic imbalance in its trade account, the small deficit did not cause much concern until the oil crisis. The trade deficit started accelerating after 1974, and Japanese *sogo-shosha* came to occupy an increasingly important place in Thailand's trade activities. Under these circumstances, General Kriangsak's regime decided to provide government subsidies to international traders under the Investment Promotion Privileges program, which had previously been given only to manufacturing firms and to some of the local trading companies. The result was the emergence of *international trading companies,* (ITCs) which policymakers conceived as a link between domestic manufacturers and foreign markets.

Requisites for Thai ITC Designation

In October 1978, the Board of Investment specified the minimum requisites for receiving the international trading company designation. These were:

1. Annual exports of 300 million bahts (about $11.1 million) during the first year, 400 million bahts in the second year, and 500 million bahts in the third year

2. Initial paid-in-capital of 30 million bahts, increasing to 50 million within three years
3. Export composition:
   a. Exports of primary exports not to exceed 100 million bahts
   b. Exports of simple processed goods, such as frozen chicken and shrimp, canned pineapples, plywood, and cotton, not to exceed 250 million bahts
   c. Minimum nontraditional exports, mostly manufactured goods, of 50 million bahts during the first year, 100 million in the second year, and 150 million in the third year
4. Public offering of stocks, or at least made available on the Stock Exchange of Thailand within five years, 75 percent of the outstanding shares to be owned by Thai citizens.

Designation of Thai ITCs

In December 1978, the Board of Investment designated four companies as ITCs: Siam Cement Trading Company, Saha Union Corporation (the former Texport International Corp., Ltd.), S.M. International Trading Company, and U.M.C. International Corporation. In 1979, seven more companies received the ITC designation: C.P. Intertrade Company, Asoke International Trading Company, International Trading Development Company, Premier International Company (the former Premier Specialties Company), Bangkok Universal Trading Company, BIS International Export Company, and Rainbow International Trading Company. Six more companies in 1980 and four more companies in 1981 also became ITCs. Thus there were altogether twenty-one applicants seeking privileges for the operation of ITCs in March 1981, when the Board of Investment temporarily closed the door for further applications, having a sufficient number of applicants. However, in June 1984, only fifteen out of twenty-one companies had started their operation and only twelve of them had received the government privileges (see table 4-9).

ITCs were typically set up as the trading arm of local conglomerates. Siam Cement International Trading Company, for example, was established with 70 percent ownership by Siam Cement Group, 10 percent by Bangkok Bank, 10 percent by Thai Farmers Bank, and 10 percent by Siam Commercial Bank. Siam Cement Group is the largest enterprise group in Thailand, with eight operating companies: The Siam Cement Co., Ltd., Siam Fiber-Cement Co., Ltd., The Concrete Products and Aggregate Co., Ltd., The Siam Iron and Steel Co., Ltd., The Siam Nowaloha Foundry Co., Ltd., The Siam Patana Estate Co., Ltd., The Thai Spare Part Co., Ltd., and The Siam International Trading Co., Ltd. In 1977, the Group had about 9,000 employees, with a net worth of 1.9 billion bahts and sales of 4.6 billion bahts. The average annual export amount during the five years between 1973 and 1977 was $120 million.

Table 4-9
Profiles of Thai ITCs, April 1984

ITC	Application Approved	Operation Started	Paid-in-Capital (millions of baht)	Total Employees
Siam Cement Trading Co., Ltd.	Dec. 18, 1978	Jan. 5, 1979	120	180
Saha Union Corp., Ltd. (Texport International Corp., Ltd.)	Dec. 18, 1978	Jan. 2, 1979	50	145
S.M. International Trading Co., Ltd.	Dec. 18, 1978	March 1980	30	45
U.M.C. International Corp., Ltd.	Dec. 18, 1978	Jan. 1982	125	100
C.P. Intertrade Co., Ltd.	March 29, 1979	July 1980	50	63
Asoke International Trading Co., Ltd.	March 29, 1979	Jan. 1981	50	150
International Trading Development Co., Ltd.	March 29, 1979	Jan. 1980		
Premier International Co., Ltd. (Premier Specialties Co., Ltd.)	March 29, 1979	Sept. 1981	30	80
Bangkok Universal Trading Co., Ltd.	June 28, 1979	July 1979		
BIS International Export Co., Ltd.	June 28, 1979	June 1981		
Rainbow International Trading Co., Ltd.	Dec. 24, 1979	Jan. 1983	30	64
Masco International Corp., Ltd.	March 27, 1980			
Mah Boonkrong Trading Co., Ltd.	March 27, 1980	Feb. 1983	50	57
River Thai International Corp., Ltd.	March 27, 1980			
Mr. Chirayoth Vasurat Vidhayakam Co., Ltd.	Sept. 12, 1980			
T&P Intertrade Corp., Ltd.	Dec. 12, 1980	July 1981	30	35
TBI Group International Trade Corp., Ltd.	Dec. 12, 1980	Feb. 1984	30	30
Chinteek Brothers (CB) International Trading Co., Ltd.	March 2, 1981	April 1984	30	13
Thai Universal Trading Co., Ltd.	March 2, 1981			
Mr. Fu Fukunchalong Co., Ltd.	March 2, 1981			
INTARICO Co., Ltd.	April 27, 1981			

Government Subsidies for Thai ITCs

To encourage exports, the government has offered both direct and indirect subsidies to Thai ITCs. Direct subsidies included tax benefits and special financing. The ITCs also benefited from numerous government support programs, originally made available to manufacturing firms, especially for energy and raw-material imports.

Direct Subsidies. The most overt government subsidies are in the form of tax benefits, including:

1. Import duty and sales-tax exemptions on raw materials and components imported to manufacture export products
2. Sales-tax exemption on raw materials and capital goods supplied by domestic producers
3. Sales-tax exemption on products supplied by domestic producers

4. Sales-tax exemption on commodities sold by domestic agents and wholesalers

5. Business-tax exemption for contracted manufacturers producing export commodities

6. Income-tax exemption on the earnings of overseas branch offices

7. Income-tax deduction for an amount equal to twice the actual export promotion expenses, such as advertising, marketing, travel, and overseas branch office operating expense, for five years

The extent of financial and foreign exchange supports from the government is not clearly known. However, ITCs are entitled to rediscount facilities for export bills, and also to maintain a foreign currency deposit account not exceeding $200,000 per year.

Indirect Subsidies. Until the early 1970s, Thailand's economic policy emphasized import substitution and regional development in an effort to take advantage of the country's large supply of natural and human resources. After the enactment of the Investment Incentives Law in 1972, there was a noticeable shift in the government's economic policy toward expansion and the development of manufacturing sector. To encourage exportation, the Investment Incentives Law permitted import duty and sales tax exemptions on raw material and capital good imports to be used in the production of export commodities, and on component imports for reexport. However, the government has not provided any support in financing or trade administration.

Performance of Thai ITCs

Eager to increase their credibility and receive government subsidies, a large number of Thai companies applied for the ITC title. However, only twelve ITCs remained in operation by April 1984. Of the ten companies that had been ITCs for at least one fiscal year by the end of 1983, only four achieved the government's export target for three years or more: Saha Union (formerly Texport International), Siam Cement Trading, C.P. Intertrade, and Asoke International Trading. U.M.C. International satisfied the minimum requisites during the first and second year of operation (1982 and 1983), while Rainbow International Trading and Mah Bookrong Trading met first year requirements in 1983. Table 4-10 gives the details of the ITCs' export performances.

Despite government subsidies and close ties with large enterprise groups, the export performance of Thai ITCs fell short of policymakers' expectations. The combined share of exports by Thai ITCs was around 1 percent of the nation's total exports in 1979 and 1980, increasing to 2.5 percent in 1981, 3.3 percent in 1982, and to 5.3 percent in 1983. These shares are far short of the comparable figures in Japan and Korea.

Table 4-10
Exports of Thai ITCs
(millions of baht)

ITC	1979	1980	1981	1982	1983	Totals
Saha Union Corp., Ltd.	637	889	1,281	1,069	1,149	5,025
Siam Cement Trading Co., Ltd.	503	643	522	610	585	2,863
S.M. International Trading Co., Ltd.			481	462	439	1,381
C.P. Intertrade Co., Ltd.		22[a]	1,130	1,342	1,378	3,872
Asoke International Trading Co., Ltd.			347	477	599	1,422
T&P Intertrade Corp., Ltd.			38[b]	259	325[c]	622
Premier International Co., Ltd.			53[d]	136	150	339
U.M.C. International Corp., Ltd.				929	2,487	3,416
Rainbow International Trading Co., Ltd.					414	414
Mah Bookrong Trading Co., Ltd.					330	330
Total	1,140	1,554	3,852	5,284	7,856	19,684
Country Total	112,151	129,709	153,036	159,630	147,892	702,418
Share (%)	1.02	1.20	2.52	3.31	5.31	2.80

Source: Department of Customs & Tarriff, *Foreign Trade Statistics of Thailand 1979–1982.*
[a]August–December only.
[b]July–December.
[c]January–July.
[d]Except May.

The ITCs could not meet the government's minimum requirement for export amount based solely on the commodities produced within their individual enterprise groups. Therefore, they sought to increase their product range by entering new businesses and by turning to previously unknown manufacturers and suppliers. Such efforts, however, suffered from ITCs' lack of experience in new business arenas and inadequate credit management. Thailand's relatively unsophisticated finance industry also created difficulties for the ITCs in effectively competing in the international trade market; Thailand's rudimentary rediscounting capability, for example, slowed down the cash cycle of exporters. In addition, the country exports generally suffered from the lack of personnel experienced in trading and the lack of quality control on the part of producers. Also the government bureaucracy tended to hinder rather than expedite the export process.[9]

Nevertheless, the ITCs can be expected to play a more prominent role in Thailand's economic process in the future; import substitution industries have already matured. Therefore, the government will have to emphasize increasingly export expansion as a vehicle for continued economic growth, and this effort will be aided by the country's vast supply of natural resources. Furthermore, with its more industrialized neighbors such as Japan, Korea, Taiwan, Singapore, and Hong Kong rapidly losing their competitive advantage in labor-intensive products, and facing greater trade restrictions in major import markets, Thailand should be able to take advantage of its large labor supply to increase exports of simple manufactured goods.

Turkish FTCCs

After following a series of import-substitution economic policies for over two decades, Turkey instituted an export promotion policy in January 1980, under the leadership of Mr. Turgut Ozal, then head of the State Planning Organization, and since 1983 prime minister. To implement the export promotion policy, the government started to provide various incentive programs to exporters, such as export financing with subsidized interests, export rebates, and tax exemptions. In 1980 the government issued a decree to designate the title of *exporter corporate company* to an export company which realized an annual export volume of $15 million or more, of which at least 50 percent must consist of manufactured or processed goods.[10]

These requirements were upgraded in 1984 to $30 million and 75 percent manufactured goods, and the title was changed to *foreign trade corporate company* (FTCC). Companies were mandated to increase export volumes by at least 10 percent annually to keep the title, and to increase capital to as much as 500 million Turkish lira (about $1.1 million as of January 1985) by the end of 1985. FTCCs were not allowed to make investments, including shares and bonds, in other companies except in export-supporting areas such as packaging of goods, warehousing, and loading.

In return for satisfying these targets and requirements, the companies designated as FTCC were entitled to special credit facilities, interest-rate reductions, and tax rebates; for instance, up to 90 percent of FTCCs' financings would be rediscounted directly by the Central Bank at interest rates much lower than commercial rates. Also, the right to handle countertrade was granted exclusively to those whose exports exceeded $50 million annually. Furthermore, these companies were given a monopoly to import from countries with centrally planned economies (COMECON countries).[11]

The number of FTCCs increased from sixteen in 1981 to twenty-one in 1984 (see table 4-11). During the same period, the contribution by FTCCs to Turkey's total exports increased from 8.1 percent to 37.5 percent, as shown in table 4-12.[12] For insight into the FTCCs, we will profile two of them: ENKA, one of the oldest and largest; and MEPTAS, one of the newest and most rapidly growing.

ENKA Marketing, Export & Import Co. Inc.
(ENKA Pazarlama Ihracat Ithalat A.S.)

ENKA Marketing was established in 1972 as the trading arm of ENKA Group, which ranked fourth among business groups in Turkey. ENKA Group had a 1983 turnover of $812 million from over 40 affiliate companies in construction, manufacturing, and trading businesses. ENKA Construction and Industry Inc. ranked first in Turkey and eleventh worldwide among construction companies in 1984.

As the largest trading company in Turkey, with exports of roughly 5 percent of the nation's total, ENKA Marketing marketed over 1,000 products to twenty-eight countries. Its 1984 exports of $328 million were highly diversified, with 29 percent in textiles, 28 percent in foodstuffs, 11 percent in chemicals, 11 percent in iron and steel products, and the rest in packing materials, automotives, electrical equipment, construction materials, and so forth. Its markets, however, were heavily skewed to Middle East countries (63 percent) due to the group's strength in construction activities in this area, while European markets took another 30 percent. Although the Far Eastern market and the U.S. market were still small, 4 percent and 3 percent, respectively, the company has moved into these areas more aggressively by establishing branch offices in Tokyo, Kuala Lumpur, Singapore, and New York. Its profit before tax stood at $4 million in 1984, about 1.3 percent of its sales.

More important than the product and market diversities, ENKA Marketing promoted exportation of products produced by companies outside the ENKA Group. In 1984, only 6 percent of its exports were internally produced, while 94 percent were purchased from outside. Also, less than 10 percent of its

Table 4-11
Profiles of Turkish FTCCs

FTCC	Date of Establishment	Capital (TL million)	Total Employees	Establishing Group	Overseas Offices	Major Product Category
AKPA	1976	50	65	4 textile companies		Textile products
ANADOLU	1981	500	100	ANADOLU Group	4	Transport vehicles, foodstuffs, chemicals
BORUSAN		500	50	BORUSAN Group	1	Steel products
CAM PQZARLAMA	1976	50	25	Turkish Glass Works		Glass-related products
COTAS	1982	530	300	COLAKOGLU Group	5	Steel products
CUKUROVA		800	70	CUKUROVA Group	6	Tractors, iron products, cement
EDPA		300	69	2 textile companies	1	Textile products
EKINCILER	1983					Iron and steel products
ENKA	1972	500	454	ENKA Group	25	Textile products, foodstuffs, chemicals
EXSA		300	77	SABANCI Group	5	Textile products, tires, cement
IMEKS	1974	500	90	DOGUS Group	4	Foodstuffs, textile products, chemicals
IZDAS		500	100	YURTCU-SIVRI Group	5	Iron and steel products, cement
MENTESOGLU		50	52	MENTESOGLU Group		Foodstuffs
MEPA	1978	500	124	Türkiye Is Bankasi	5	Foodstuffs, textiles, construction materials
MEPTAS	1982	50	42	METAS Group	3	Iron and steel products
PENTA	1976					
RAM	1970	50	174	KOC Group		Industrial products, consumer goods
SÜZER	1979	250	101	SÜZER Group	2	Foodstuffs
TEKFEN	1981	500	98	TEKFEN Group	16	Iron and steel products, construction mater
TEMEL	1983	500	35	STFA Group	6	Construction materials
YASAR	1971	500	143	YASAR Group	1	Textile products, foodstuffs

Table 4-12
Exports of Turkish FTCCs
(millions of dollars)

FTCC	1981	1982	1983	1984
AKPA	51	94	123	114
ANADOLU	3	19	55	176
BORUSAN	10	20	46	54
CAM PAZARLAMA	36	38	67	111
COTAS				67
CUKUROVA	13	80	83	86
EDPA	8	50	88	150
EKINCILER			14	51
ENKA	85	193	312	341
EXSA	40	83	119	178
IMEKS	2	6	43	102
IZDAS	8	37	66	71
MENTESOGLU	20	51	119	149
MEPA	11	26	118	210
MEPTAS			29	68
PENTA				61
RAM	65	113	180	220
SÜZER	11	19	38	110
TEKFEN	1	19	54	132
TEMEL			22	70
YASAR	11	56	87	102
Total	381	930	1,665	2,623
Country Total	4,703	5,746	5,728	7,000[a]
Share (%)	8.1	16.2	29.1	37.5

[a]Estimated

exports were made by a paper transaction of an exportation already accomplished by smaller sized trading firms, an ill-advised technique that FTCCs frequently practiced to benefit from high export rebates (5.5 percent to FTCCs compared to up to 2.64 percent to those exporting less than $10 million).[13]

Facing stiffer competition from other FTCCs in export markets for the same export items, ENKA Marketing in 1984 decided to move to upstream activities in trading by purchasing directly from producers and storing products. Grain elevators with 200,000 ton capacity were constructed in Eastern Turkey. This was expected to result in more emphasis on commodities and raw materials, an area in which Japanese *sogo-shosha* had traditional strengths. ENKA Marketing also increased import business (to $150 million in 1984) by consolidating the group's import requirements and third-country trade ($90 million in 1984) to accommodate increasing demand for countertrade by COMECON countries.

An executive of ENKA Marketing explained these changes as a natural outcome of ENKA's basic policy to move to new areas of business constantly, since the number one position in the export business could be easily lost to newcomers due to low entry barriers in the trading business, and to the government's attitude not to favor large enterprises. These policy changes also reflected the company's long-term objective to become a full-fledged general trading company.

MEPTAS (Manisali Evrensel Pazarlama ve Ticaret A.S.)

MEPTAS was established in 1982 as the trading arm of the Ege Yatirim and METAS Group, which was the oldest industrial group and leading producer of steel and iron products in Turkey. The group's turnover reached $165 million in 1984 through its twenty-one affiliate companies.

With exports of $30 million in 1983, MEPTAS was designated as the nineteenth FTCC. Then it more than doubled its exports to $68 million in 1984. Major items exported by MEPTAS were iron and steel products (45 percent) and textile and leather goods (20 percent), as well as a substantial amount of machinery and foodstuffs. Like ENKA, MEPTAS heavily depended on the Middle Eastern market (for 70 percent of its business) and on European countries (25 percent), but it also exported steel products to the U.S. market, which was expected to grow rapidly because of the captive supply of quality steel products by METAS Group companies. The group also owned transportation companies (trucking and shipping agencies) and warehouses to complement export activities by MEPTAS.

U.S. ETCs

The United States is the vanguard of free trade policies in the world. However, chronic trade deficits since 1973 have prompted the U.S. government to search for ways to help remedy the trade problem. One solution that it tried was to form the *export trading company* (ETC), a U.S. version of the GTC.

Two institutional barriers have hindered exports by U.S. firms. First, since the Great Depression, there has been a clear demarcation between banking and commerce, which has kept many commercial banks from playing active roles in the international growth of their clients. Also, the International Banking Act of 1978 gave the Federal Reserve Bank System firm controls over the nontraditional banking activities of both domestic and foreign banks in the United States.

The second barrier has been antitrust legislation. The law's intent was to promote competition within the U.S. economy, but extraterritorial application of antitrust laws often lessened U.S. exporters' competitiveness in the international trade arena, where successful penetration of foreign markets requires exporters to handle even ostensibly competing lines of goods.

These institutional barriers to exportation are not a new problem. In 1916, the Federal Trade Commission produced a report stating that "U.S. companies were at a serious disadvantage in the overseas markets, due to the strong cartels that existed among other nations' industries."[14] This report led Congress to enact the Webb-Pomerene Act of 1918, officially called the Export Trade Act.

The Webb-Pomerene Act exempted export trade associations from some prohibition of the Sherman and Clayton Acts so long as they did not interfere with domestic competition. But the statutory vagueness of the Act left a threat of subsequent antitrust litigation by the Justice Department and the Federal Trade Commission against trade associations. Furthermore, the Webb-Pomerene Act did not extend its antitrust exemption to service exports, such as consulting, engineering, construction, insurance, finance, and other invisible trade, of industries whose growth has accelerated during the last few decades to account for some 65 percent of the gross national product of the United States.

During the late 1970s, as the United States faced increased pressure from Japanese exporters, many decisionmakers in Washington became interested in the ways that Japanese *sogo-shosha* had accelerated the growth of their nation's exports. The Department of Commerce had been interested in modelling after the Japanese system for a long time, and Senators Adlai Stevenson III, John Glenn, John Heinz, and John Danforth had actively promoted the idea. Their concerted interest led to the Stevenson-Heinz Version, which passed the Senate in September 1980. Various regional banks, the Chamber of Commerce, and Port Authorities of Northeastern States actively lobbied for the bill. Congress passed the bill in August 1982. But then, the Attorney General's Office and the Federal Reserve Board called a balk against the bill on the grounds of its conflict with the Antitrust Act and the existing banking system. Finally, the huge trade deficit of nearly $30 billion per year coupled with the high unemployment rate of 10.1 precent at the time persuaded President Reagan to sign the bill into law on October 8, 1982.

The Export Trading Company Act of 1982 consists of four titles. (See appendix B for the complete text of the law.) Title I describes the general provisions, declaring the purpose of the act and defining the terms. Title II, the "Bank Export Services Act," modifies existing banking laws to allow bank ownership and investment in ETCs. Title III, "Export Trade Certificates of Review," and Title IV, "Foreign Trade Antitrust Improvements Act," give exporters greater freedom from antitrust concerns.

The Export Trading Company Defined

Title I of the Export Trading Company Act defines an ETC as "a person, partnership, association, or similar organization, whether operated for profit or as a nonprofit organization, . . . which is organized and operated principally [to export] goods or services produced in the United States, or [to facilitate] the exportation . . . by providing export trade services." Export goods refer to tangible property manufactured, produced, grown, or extracted in the United States, with the cost of imported raw materials and components not exceeding 50 percent of sales price. Service exports include "accounting, amusement, architectural, automatic data processing, business, communications, construction franchising and licensing, consulting, engineering, financial, insurance, legal, management, repair, tourism, training, and transportation services." In the case of services, at least 50 percent of the sales or billings price must be provided by U.S. citizens or be otherwise attributable to the United States. Finally, export trade services include "consulting, international market research, marketing, insurance, product research and design, legal assistance, transportation, including trade documentation and freight forwarding, communication and processing of foreign orders to and for exporters and foreign purchasers, warehousing, foreign exchange, financing, and taking title to goods."[15]

Support to ETCs

Prior to the ETC Act, the U.S. government's export assistance was limited to measures such as special tax benefits to Domestic International Sales Corporations (DISCs),[16] low-cost Exim bank financing, insurance against financial risks including expropriation and inability to collect export bills, the gathering of overseas marketing information for would-be exporters, and some specialized support programs for exporters of weapons and agricultural goods.

The ETC Act did not so much institute specific subsidies for would-be exporters as remove impediments, particularly in the banking and antitrust areas, to the formation of export-oriented trading companies. The act provided two important features to ETCs. First, it allowed a bank to hold ownership in ETCs, even majority interest, as long as its total investment did not exceed 5 percent of its own consolidated capital and surplus (Title II, Sec. 203).

Second, the act generally exempted ETCs from antitrust legislation as long as they did not unreasonably lessen or restrain commerce in the United States. Title III specifically provided general exemption from criminal and civil antitrust actions for ETCs that received certificates from the Department of Commerce. This removed the concerns that would-be exporters following the Webb-Pomerene Act had against possible prosecution by the Justice Department and the Federal Trade Commission. Title IV amended the Sherman Act and the Federal Trade Commission Act, so that ETCs' export transactions would not be challenged on the antitrust grounds as long as they did not substantially or foreseeably harm U.S. consumers or competitors.

In addition, the ETC Act called on the Department of Commerce to create an office for actively promoting the formation and operation of ETCs (Title I, Sec. 104).[17] Trade financing through the Exim bank was also increased to support the development of ETCs (Title II, Sec. 206).[18]

The Expectation for the ETC

The ETC bill had been expected to improve the country's troubled balance of trade. Because of a large domestic market, there has been a general lack of export-orientation in the United States, particularly among small- to medium-sized manufacturers, who considered international trade to be too risky and cumbersome to be profitable. The primary driving force behind the ETC Act was the need for a trade entity that could provide the full range of services required to link U.S. suppliers with overseas consumers.

Unlike the existing small export management companies (EMCs), which were too small to achieve economies of scale in international markets and which offered only fragmented trade services, ETCs were conceived as U.S.-based trading entities that would handle multiproduct links with a complete package of export services from market research to trade financing. Such entities would enable small manufacturing firms to make only "one stop" to export their products, greatly reducing the expense and expertise required in international trade.

The ETC bill brought with it high hopes for increased GNP and lower trade deficits in the U.S. economy. Chase Econometrics, for example, released a study in August 1981 called "The Macroeconomic Impact of Authorizing U.S. Export Trading Companies," which predicted that "between 320,000 and 640,000 new jobs could be created by 1985 . . . as much as $55 billion might be added to the gross national product by that year, and $11 billion to $22 billion could be lopped off the federal deficit." In summarizing the results, the report said, "There is substantial evidence that the lack of export trading companies in the United States is a significant reason for the relatively slow growth in foreign trade. Authorizing [ETCs] would have a powerful, positive effect upon the American economy."[19] Although the projection was later revised downward to 275,000 new jobs, $22 billion to GNP, $9 billion off the federal deficit, and nearly $11 billion additional net exports of goods and services, the new figures were substantial enough to impress the people concerned.[20] Senator Heinz, one of the key actors in shepherding the bill through Congress, also urged chief executive officers of America's banks to examine the possibility of forming ETCs because "it is entirely possible that 20 years from now, American export trading companies may have market power and financial relevance comparable to those of other countries," such as Japan.[21]

In spite of such an optimistic view by econometricians and policymakers, scholars' opinions of the ETC Act varied. Professor Phillip Grub of George

Washington University expected that bank ownership of ETCs would prove successful in promoting exports.[22] In contrast, Professor Gail Oxley of Stanford commented that a perception of almost limitless opportunity for growth and profits in the domestic market would continue to serve as a disincentive for exports.[23] Professor Yoshi Tsurumi of Baruch College hinted that the ETC Act could be not more than a disguised attempt to remove barriers to interstate commerce.[24]

Alden Abbott of the Justice Department went so far as to suggest that the ETC Act "actually imposes new regulatory encumbrances or trading company activities" as "Congress has unwittingly jeopardized the antitrust protection enjoyed by U.S. firms doing business abroad," and "Title IV may offer the most antitrust protection not to U.S. exporters, but to foreign firms doing business abroad."[25]

The real answer to whether the ETC will be an effective vehicle for promoting the U.S. exports lies in the attitude of managers, who are the potential customers of the export services of the ETCs. American managers, especially in small- to medium-sized manufacturing companies, are oriented primarily toward the domestic market. Also, they tend to emphasize short-term profit to the detriment of building market share, in contrast with Japanese management's long-term effort to build a solid foundation in overseas markets.[26] The crux of the question, therefore, is whether the U.S. managers can appreciate long-term interests in establishing a presence in foreign markets, which is a necessary condition for developing a GTC.

Even if the attitudinal inertia of American management changes, the 1981 study by Chase Econometrics seems too optimistic. The United States has been exporting annually more than $200 billion worth of goods and services, which have been handled by four types of business entity: roughly 15 percent has been handled by giant commodity traders such as Phillip Brothers division of Phibro Corp., Cargill, and Continental Grain; 6 percent has been handled by more than 1,100 export management companies; 10 percent has been handled by foreign trading companies mostly based in Japan;[27] and over two-thirds of exports have been handled directly by manufacturers. ETCs, therefore, will have to compete with these entities to make inroads to U.S. export activities. Given the size and maturity of the U.S. economy, it is not an easy task for the ETCs to have an immediate and sizable impact.

Establishment of ETCs

As of June 1984, there were 349 ETCs in the United States, including 46 in California and 43 in New York, according to *Export Trading Companies, Contract Facilitation Service Directory* published by the U.S. Department of Commerce.[28] The list of these 349 ETCs is shown in appendix C. Not all ETCs, however, have the same status. Thirty-one ETCs received the Federal Reserve

Certificate based on the Banking Provision of Title II as of January 1985. Forty-five ETCs received the Commerce Certificate based on the Antitrust Provision of Title III. Among these, General Electric Trading Company and Sears World Trade Company stand out as two major ETCs. Let us review the profiles of these two companies to understand the ETC system more clearly.

General Electric Trading Company (GETC). GETC was established in March 1982 as a wholly owned subsidiary of General Electric (GE), one of the most diversified of U.S. multinational corporations. In 1984 GE had sales of $27.9 billion and a worldwide sales office network in 55 countries.[29] Its exports amounted to $4.0 billion, making it the fourth largest exporter among U.S. industrial corporations.[30] More important, GE is known for its innovative strategy development and implementation processes, providing a standard example to policy text books and other firms.

GETC's major objective is to assist various GE strategic business units engaged in export activities, by consolidating their countertrade requirements. These requirements, which a government imposes on importers to buy goods from its country as a condition for selling in its country, have become a prevalent form of international trade. Countertrade's volume in world trade has grown from 2 percent in 1976, to 20 percent in 1979, and to 30 percent, or $600 billion, in 1984. It is this author's belief that it was coincidental, therefore, that GETC was established in 1982, the year that the Export Trading Company Act was enacted in the United States. Indeed, GETC would have been established regardless of the passage of the act.

GETC was formed in three sections: sales and marketing, finance, and international-trade development. The finance operation supports the business sections within GETC by financing projects and credit checking customers. Sales and marketing first exported goods produced by smaller American firms, but was later dissolved. International-trade development is responsible for actual business operation. It is divided into seven sections. The first five sections deal with product trading areas—machinery; metals and materials; electrical; chemicals, oil and construction materials; and industrial products. The last two sections are the advanced trading section, responsible for initiating projects and organizing various functions to materialize them; and the countertrade and barter section, responsible for all countertrade and barter proposals and contract maintenance for active projects.

GETC's turnover grew to $160 million in 1984. Its 1987 volume was projected to reach $1 billion.[31] In spite of such rapid growth, the company has chosen a conservative approach, slowly expanding the number of traders to 80 during the same period. As an executive of the company put it, GETC made a conscious effort not to "overreach,"[32] a pattern that most trading companies are likely to fall into given the nature of the trading business.

Thus far, GETC has generated its business through the GE system, rather than creating new supplier and customer bases independent of GE's business lines. For example, GETC's plan called for one-third of its business on electrical, mechanical, and industrial products to be generated from outside customers, but all of these businesses were expected to complement GE's own products so that they could be packaged together for exportation.[33] GETC remains a trading company dealing mostly with GE-related countertrade and barter, with no immediate plan to deviate itself from this mode. But with the accumulation of expertise in the trade business, GETC's long-term perspective may be to move toward becoming a full-fledged general trading company providing comprehensive export-related services to independent suppliers and customers.

Sears World Trade Inc. Sears World Trade Inc. (SWT) was established in October 1982 as a wholly owned subsidiary of Sears Roebuck & Co. The giant retailer had previous export operations and perceived an opportunity to become a premier U.S. trading company by forming a one-stop, general trading firm similar to the Japanese *sogo-shosha*. Its fifty-nine-year retail merchandising experience gave the new subsidiary advantages including a strong network of foreign and domestic sources for consumer goods, broad expertise in consumer products and product development, financial strength and capital-raising expertise, and an international distribution network and foreign buying offices.[34]

SWT was created with the mission of becoming a "truly significant factor in world trade" by offering a complete portfolio of capabilities in trading, trade finance, and business consulting.[35] Five primary business-development strategies were announced. These encompassed technology and management services, imports into the United States, third-country trade, countertrade, and exports from the United States.[36] Unlike the more narrowly focused General Electric Trading Company, SWT was intended to deal in virtually any kind of goods and services, much like the Japanese *sogo-shosha*.[37] However, it was not a mere emulation since, in contrast to the traditional high-volume, low-margin Japanese operation, SWT expected to be a high-value-added business and had no intention of becoming either a major commodity importer or the principal international purchasing agent of its parent.[38]

The firm was originally organized into three operating groups. A general-trading arm concentrated on consumer products, technology transfer, agribusiness, and health care. A technical-services group offered specialized trade research and trade-related management consulting. A financial-services operation was charged with finding "innovative" funding for SWT clients.[39] The firm's top officers included an impressive line-up of former government officials, and the staff, who were former Sears buyers, export managers, and marketing people, were viewed "as a nucleus for expansion." In 1984 the company had 1,000 employees and 42 offices in 15 countries.[40]

The initial prformance of SWT, however, was somewhat less than impressive. In 1983, its first full operating year, it posted a $12.1 million loss on $79.1 million revenue.[41] Its original chairman was replaced and a major reassessment of the company made. The crux of the problem seemed to lie in SWT's failure to establish a clear, consistent strategic plan.[42] In fact, much of the revenue, instead of coming from the actual business of trading, came from a series of acquisitions and joint ventures that supported the main line of business. These included Harbridge House, a Boston management consulting firm; Price & Pierce Group Ltd., the world's leading agent of forest products; Sears First Chicago Trading, the first ETC formed by a bank and nonbank; Sears-Schenkers Services, a joint venture with a Frankfurt freight forwarder; and other tie-ups with Italian and Philippine trading and consulting firms.[43] Also, management's insistence on improving margins by adding value to each deal prompted it to engage in all kinds of products and activities. The rationale was management's belief that the more business that SWT did, the more possibilities for adding value. The result was overextension and an organizational disarray that has kept SWT from getting off the ground.

The management, led by a new chairman Richard M. Jones, has set about trying to turn SWT around. Concrete plans are being deliberated for integrating the trading company with the international buying arm of Sears' merchandising group, and concentrating more on the consumer goods business.

Trading Companies Compared

Table 4-13 compares general trading companies or their equivalents in six countries. Although all of these companies are expected to promote the exports of their countries, their profiles are as different as their names. Korea (until 1978) and Thailand have the most extensive requisites, while the U.S. government has no specific requisites for designating ETCs. The most popular forms of requisites are minimum exports, minimum capital, and export item diversity, while market diversity, public stock offering, and ownership control are required in some countries.

In most countries, incentive systems are offered to compensate for the burden of satisfying the requisites; thus the extent of the incentives parallels the extent of the requisites. Preferential financing and tax benefits are offered in every country except in the United States, while ease of administrative burdens and special treatment in foreign exchange are exercised in a few countries. Import privilege was given in Korea and in Japan in the early periods of their GTCs.

The number of GTCs in each country varies greatly, ranging from over 360 in the United States to 5 in Taiwan. It is interesting to observe that the number of GTCs in two countries with the most successful performances, namely Japan and Korea, coincide at 9 after a certain variation in the past.

Table 4-13
GTCs Compared by Country, End of 1984

	Japan	Korea	Taiwan	Thailand	Turkey	USA
GTC name[a]	Sogo-Shosha	General trading company	Large trading company	International trading company	Foreign trade corporate company	Export trading company
Year started	1870s[b]	1975	1978	1978	1980	1982
Requisites	No requisites					
Minimum exports		*	*	*	*	
Item diversity		c		*	*	
Market diversity		c	*	*	*	
Minimum capital		c	*	*		
Public stock offering		*		*		
Ownership control		*	*	*		* (restrictions reduced)
Incentives						
Preferential financing		*	*	*	*	
Tax benefits	*	*	*	*	*	
Ease of administrative burdens		*				*
Special treat in foreign exchange		*		*		
Import privilege	* (1950s)	*			*	

	9	9[d]	5	21 (6 operating)	21	349
Number of GTCs						
Ownership						
Business group	*(all 9)	*(8)			*	
Bank			*	*		*
Trader			*	*		*
Manufacturer			*			*
Government		*(1)				*
Average exports per GTC ($ million)	7,871.5 (1984)	1,241.8 (1983)	53.04 (1982)	34.16 (1983)	124.9 (1984)	NA
GTCs' combined share of national exports	41.7% (1984)	51.3% (1983)	1.19% (1982)	5.31% (1983)	37.5% (1984)	NA

*means specific requisites or incentives designated by the respective government.

[a]The names of GTC quoted are the English version of the official names used in respective countries. The Japanese case is the only exception to this rule, as her local name "sogo-shosha" is internationally used and understood.

[b]The term sogo-shosha was coined in the late 1950s.

[c]These requisites were deleted in 1978.

[d]The number of Korea's GTCs was reduced from 10 to 9 in 1984 with the dropout of Kumho Trading.

The most popular form of GTC ownership is the business group, dominant in Japan, Korea, Thailand, and Turkey. Bank ownership is next in order, as shown in Taiwan, Thailand and the United States. Traders, manufacturers, and national and local governments also participate in the GTC industry.

Given the short time span that has elapsed since the creation of the GTCs in many countries, it is too early to draw sweeping conclusions from a comparison of their export performances. Yet some observations can be attempted. Fully diversified trading companies have yet to be developed in countries other than Japan. Present-day trading companies in Korea show limited diversification compared to Japanese *sogo-shosha*. They are in fact little more than large trading companies, comparable only to Japanese trading companies of the early 1960s. Yet Korea has most closely emulated the Japanese GTC system, followed only by Turkish companies. The combined share of the nine Korean GTCs constituted 51.3 percent of the nation's total exports in 1983, surpassing the share of nine *sogo-shosha,* which stood at 41.7 percent in 1984. Although larger in number, twenty-one Turkish FTCCs also come close to these two leaders, with an export share of 37.5 percent in 1984.

The GTCs of Korea and Turkey, like the Japanese *sogo-shosha,* have benefited greatly from the support of large business groups and the readily accessible suppliers within these groups. Government-operated GTCs and GTCs backed by banks have not yet shown such success. Taiwanese and Thai GTCs are not yet established as significant factors in their respective export industries, exporting less than a few percentage points of their national totals. The statistics for the U.S. ETCs are not yet available, but the early hope on these entities has undoubtedly withered.

These comparisons explain some of the reasons why certain GTCs performed less effectively than others. In Taiwan, the LTCs did not have enough driving force within themselves for promoting exports. Banks, small- and medium-sized traders, and manufacturers could not be as effective as large business groups in generating large volume items for exportation. In Thailand, the bottlenecks to export growth seem to be the lack of export items with sufficient international competitiveness. Vehicles for exportation such as GTC can work only when the competitive export items exist. It is interesting to note that the success of GTCs in Japan, an advanced country; Korea, a newly industrializing country; and Turkey, a developing country, does not seem to be related to the countries' stages of economic development.

It is premature to predict either the success or failure of the U.S. ETCs. Application of the experiences of other countries can be misleading because of the substantial differences between the U.S. economy and others. Yet, one can speculate that ETCs will have tougher tasks than any other GTCs in the world in making inroads in the export industry because of the relative inexperience in the export business by U.S. managers, and the existence of substitutive channels in the form of formidable manufacturing-oriented multinational corporations.

Notes

1. Yoshi Tsurumi, *Sogo-shosha: Engines of Export-based Growth* (Montreal: The Institute for Research on Public Policy, 1980), 21.
2. Alexander K. Young, *The Sogo Shosha: Japan's Multinational Trading Companies* (Boulder, Colo.: Westview Press, 1979), 84. Kanematsu and Gosho—both strong in textiles—were merged in 1967. Nissho and Iwai—both strong in metals— were merged in 1968. Ataka was dissolved in 1977, and its steel business along with several other areas were taken over by C. Itoh.
3. Kunio Yoshihara, *Sogo-shosha: The Vanguard of the Japanese Economy* (Tokyo: Oxford University Press, 1983), 150-151.
4. Ibid., p. 119.
5. Nikkei Business, ed., *Shosha; Huyu no Zidai* (Trading Companies; Age of Winter)(Nihon Keizai Shinboong Sha, 1983), 1-2.
6. Ryuzo Sejima, former chairman of C. Itoh & Co., interview with the author, March 17, 1981, in Dong-Sung Cho, *Hankook-eui Chonghapmooyuk-Sangsa, Sang: Bonjil-kwa Cheonryak* (Korea's General Trading Companies, Vol. II: Concept and Strategy)(Beopmoonsa, 1983), 344-353.
7. This section is abstracted from Dong-Sung Cho, "The Anatomy of Korean General Trading Companies," *Journal of Business Research* 12, no. 2 (1984):241-255.
8. "Taiwan's Big Companies Still No Match for Japanese Giants," *Business Asia* (September 24, 1982), 12.
9. Kheeseng Anansiriprapha, "General Trading Companies and Manufactured Exports from Thailand," Master's thesis, Thammasat University, Bangkok, May 1983, 173-174.
10. This section benefited from comments by Mustafa Ozel, research director, Foreign Trade Association of Turkey.
11. Since 1985, export financing by the government to any exporters, including FTCCs, has ended. At the same time, the privilege of countertrade has been allowed to all exporters.
12. Based on data compiled by Mr. Mustafa Ozel, research director, Foreign Trade Association of Turkey.
13. Up to $2 million, there is no export rebate. For the next $8 million, the rebate is 3.3 percent. Thus the maximum effective rate is 3.3 percent of the incremental $8 million, or 80 percent of the total exports resulting in 2.64 percent.
14. "The Export Trading Company Act," *International Banker* (February 17, 1983): 19.
15. See appendix B for the complete text of the law.
16. DISCs are paper organizations that nominally handle exports. By setting up a DISC, a manufacturer can defer taxes indefinitely up to 50 percent of export earnings. As of April 1984, there were about 17,000 U.S. companies taking advantage of this tax break. See, for more details of DISC and the complaints of European manufacturers against them, *Fortune* (April 2, 1984): 66.
17. Based on the ETC Act, the Office of Export Company Affairs was established by the Commerce Department. Its location is Room 6711, US Department of Commerce, 14th & Constitution Avenue, N.W., Washington, D.C. 20230.
18. For more detailed descriptions of the ETC Act, refer to the following two articles: Tom Becker and James L. Porter, "Selling, ETC," *S&MM* (July 4, 1983): 44-48;

and Alden Abbot, "Missing the Boat on Export Trading Companies," *Regulation* (November/December 1982): 39-44.

19. "The Export Trading Company Act," *International Banker* (February 17, 1983): 14.

20. Ibid., 14.

21. Ibid., 12.

22. Phillip Grub, telephone conversation with the author, March 4, 1981.

23. Gail Oxley, interview with the author, March 11, 1981.

24. Yoshi Tsurumi, interview with the author, March 3, 1981.

25. Abbot, "Missing the Boat," 39-44.

26. Philip Maher, "Trading Companies: A US Export Panacea?", *International Marketing* (October 1982): 62.

27. Regarding the performance of the Japanese *sogo-shosha* as exporters from the United States, see "Unlikely American Exporter: Japan," *Wall Street Journal,* international ed. (November 11, 1981): 10. For the breakdown of U.S. exports by agents, see "The Export Trading Company Act," *International Banker* (February 17, 1983): 26.

28. *Export Trading Companies, Contract Facilitation Service Directory,* US Department of Commerce, International Trade Administration, June 1984.

29. General Electric Trading Company, personal correspondence with the author, May, 1985.

30. *Fortune* (August 6, 1984): 37.

31. In May 1985, GETC revised its 1987 sales projection to $1 billion from $2 billion as reported in *International Management* (January 1984): 16.

32. M. A. Pawluk, "How One Company Manages Its Countertrade," Remarks to International Symposium on Development in International Trade and Export Incentives, Istanbul, Turkey, January 16, 1985.

33. "Here Come the U.S. Trading Firms," *International Management* (January 1984): 18.

34. "The Export Trading Company Act," *International Banker* (February 17, 1983): 29.

35. "Sears' Humbled Trading Empire," *Fortune* (June 25, 1983): 29.

36. "The Export Trading Company Act," *International Banker* (February 17, 1983): 29.

37. Ibid., 28.

38. "Sears Trades on a Name," *Industry Week* (March 19, 1984): 83.

39. Ibid., 83.

40. "A Costly Startup for Sears World Trade," *International Management* (September 1984): 8.

41. "Sears Trades on a Name," *Industry Week* (March 19, 1984): 83.

42. "Sears' Humbled Trading Empire," 72.

43. "A Costly Startup for Sears World Trade," *International Management* (September 1984): 8.

5
Generic Strategies of the Trading Company

his chapter compares the basic strategies for growth available to the managers of trading companies. The strategies are shown schematically in figure 5-1, in which the three dimensions represent product, area, and functional diversification, respectively.[1] Each of the eight corners in the hexahedron represents a basic strategy for growth. This chapter examines and evaluates the eight generic diversification strategies available to trading companies.

Strategy A: Complete Specialization

Under strategy A, a trading company pursues specialization in product, area, and function. It is assumed that exportation is the basic function for any functionally specialized trading company.

Advantage: High Efficiency. Any business entity, small or large, has a limited availability of human and capital resources. Therefore, its financial performance will depend on management's ability to allocate the limited resources for maximum efficiency. One solution is to concentrate the company's resources in the segment with the highest potential profitability, rather than dividing the resources in a large number of products, areas, or functions. Complete specialization may bring high efficiency.

Disadvantage: Limited Growth. A trading company that handles an internationally competitive product will be able to sell that product in new markets as well as in its traditional market. Similarly, a company that has established a monopoly position in a market for its traditional product may be able to sell other products by taking advantage of its market expertise, including its knowledge of the local distribution network and government. A company that pursues a complete specialization strategy is, in effect, foregoing the possibility of incremental growth and profit.

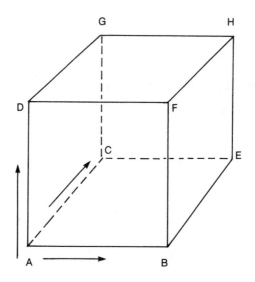

Strategy	Product	Area	Function
A	Specialization	Specialization	Specialization
B	Diversification	Specialization	Specialization
C	Specialization	Diversification	Specialization
D	Specialization	Specialization	Diversification
E	Diversification	Diversification	Specialization
F	Diversification	Specialization	Diversification
G	Specialization	Diversification	Diversification
H	Diversification	Diversification	Diversification

Figure 5-1. Generic Strategies for Growth Available to Trading Companies

Evaluation. Strategy A offers high profitability in return for limited growth potential. While this strategy is simple conceptually, its actual implementation is problematic. To begin with, it is difficult to identify the market or the product in which a trading company should specialize for maximum efficiency. Furthermore, profitability, which is most often used as a measure of efficiency, is not easily or uniformly defined. Some prefer to use absolute measures such as gross income, operating income, or net income, while others use proportional measures such as gross margin, operating margin, or net margin as indicators of profitability.

Under strategy A, managers of a trading company must make investment decisions on the product to be exported or the market to be developed prior to any actual transaction. The company selects and invests in a specialized segment, which it believes to be the high profitability segment, and then enters into contracts to export a certain product to a certain market. There is often a considerable lag between signing a contract and realizing profits; some contracts may take months and even years before they are consummated. Trading contracts generally include expected (a priori) profit margins for the trading company, but there is no guarantee that such margins will actually be realized; any unforeseen changes in demand or supply conditions can affect the eventual (a posteriori) profitability of a contract.

A trading company, therefore, is forced to make its trading decision on the basis of its expectation of profit. The relationship between a priori and a posteriori profits can be summarized as follows:

$$R = r \cdot P(r)$$

where

$R =$ a posteriori profit
$r =$ priori profit
$P(r) =$ the probability that a priori profit will be realized.

A posteriori profitability is a function of two independent variables, a priori profitability and the probability that a priori profitability will be realized. The second independent variable, $P(r)$, captures the risk factor in a trading decision: the higher the probability that a priori profitability will be realized, the lower the risk involved. This relationship between risk and return can be presented schematically as in figure 5-2[2]. Barrier to entry is represented on the vertical axis, and barrier to exit on the horizontal axis. Barrier to entry is the ease or difficulty with which a potential competitor can enter an industry. The height of this barrier depends on a variety of factors, including availability of technological expertise, level of minimum capital investment required, and

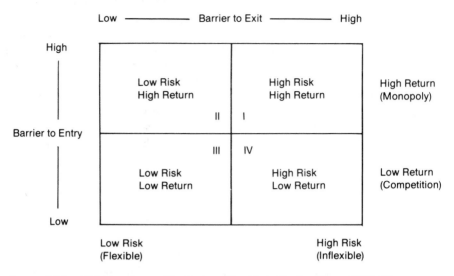

Source: Michael F. Porter, *Competitive Strategy* (New York: The Free Press, 1980), 22.

Figure 5-2. Risk and Return Matrix

possibility of capturing a certain minimum share of the market for profitable operation. Barrier to exit is the ability of a company in a particular industry to withdraw from that industry. Again, this barrier depends on a number of considerations, such as the remaining useful life of fixed assets and technological expertise, transferability or dismissal of employees, and the impact on the company's image.

In the schematic model presented in figure 5-2, barrier to entry reflects the profitability, and barrier to exit the risk factor, present in an industry. The higher the barrier to entry, the smaller the number of competitors in the industry, with consequent opportunities for higher profits. In contrast, the lower the barriers to entry, the greater the number of competitors, and the lower the profitability. The height of the barrier to exit reflects the degree of risk involved. Following a faulty investment decision, a company may decide to divest its unprofitable operation in a particular industry. However, if the barrier to exit is high in that industry, the company runs the risk of being forced to continue its operation in spite of losses.

The first quadrant in figure 5-2 represents industries with both high return and high risk. Foremost among such industries are steel, petroleum, and petrochemicals, which require large initial investments. At the same time, even if the operation is unprofitable, exit from the industry is made difficult by the large volume of fixed assets which would have to be disposed of. In some instances, government policy may not permit a company to abandon its operations in what are often considered industries vital to national security and welfare.

The second quadrant represents industries with high return and low risk, such as information and technology service industries. To operate in such industries, a company must invest considerable time and human resources to establish its reputation. However, once it is established, competition from newcomers tends to be limited. At the same time, exit from such industries tends to be relatively easy. Industries that often require government license or designation, such as mineral extraction or harbor loading and unloading, can also be included in the category of high-return, low-risk industries.

The third quadrant represents industries with both low return and low risk, where both barriers to entry and to exit tend to be low. Domestic commerce and trade agencies can be considered to be this low-return, low-risk category. The fourth quadrant represents industries with low return and high risk. Industries which require little initial capital investment but high labor concentration generally fall into this category.

A trading company that chooses to pursue strategy A can apply this risk-return analysis to select its specialization segment. The company's goal is to participate in a segment with high barrier to entry and low barrier to exit, thereby enjoying high return and low risk.

Strategy B: Product Diversification

Under strategy B, a trading company pursues product diversification, but continues to specialize in area and function.

Advantages. Continued area specialization offers the possibility of the following benefits:

Country Representation in a Specialized Area. By developing expertise in a certain foreign market, a trading company can serve as the export window for all manufacturing firms of its own country in that specialized area. Among European trading houses, Internatio Mueller once represented the Netherlands in the Caribbean; United Africa Co. represented England in Anglophone Africa; and SCOA represented France in Nigeria. Of Korean GTCs, Daewoo serves as the primary exporter of Korean products to Libya and Sudan, Hyundai to Iraq, and Hyosung to Taiwan.

Increased Value-Added. Specialization in one area may permit a trading company to participate directly in the local distribution process, thus increasing its value-added by controlling a large portion of the trade process.

Use of an Established Distribution Network. Once a company penetrates a foreign market, it can gradually develop distribution networks that can be used to distribute other products. For example, Korean companies such as Goldstar and Samsung entered the U.S. market by supplying color television sets to discount stores and by establishing their own distribution networks, which were later used to sell other electronic products such as microwave ovens and VCRs.[3]

Comparative Advantage over Manufacturers. Manufacturing firms generally cannot develop the level of market knowledge that is available to trading companies. Just as manufacturers' expertise is in the product, trading companies' expertise is in the market. Therefore, trading companies can often sell products in a foreign market that is beyond the reach of manufacturing firms. For example, Korea's Goldstar could not market its television sets independently in Iraq, and turned to Hyundai, which had developed an expertise in the Iraqi market.

Disadvantages. Continued area specialization has the following potential disadvantages:

Small Market Size. Foreign trading companies can establish dominant market positions only in small economies. Large markets such as in the United States or Europe tend to be extremely competitive, and therefore there is little opportunity for a single trading company to establish monopolistic market power, let alone maintain a dominant market position.

Limited Growth Potential. In a small economy, a trading company can easily saturate the market, rapidly exhausting opportunities for continued growth.

High Country Risk. Companies often establish their positions in a foreign market by developing a close relationship with, and gaining special favors from, the incumbent government. This is particularly true in less-developed countries. The political environment in such economies, however, tends to be relatively unstable, and any change in the government leadership, or even the reassignment of key government officials, can effectively undermine relationships that a company may have cultivated. Korea's Hyosung, for example, had a large share of Iran's tire market. The recent change in Iran's political leadership and the war with Iraq, therefore, greatly reduced Hyosung's operations.

Evaluation. Despite its shortcomings, strategy B is a valuable strategy for growth. It is particularly appropriate for a trading company that has the support of a relatively small business group with limited capabilities. Empirical analyses suggest that there is an inverse relationship between area diversification and profitability; area diversification can lead to an overextension of a company's resources, resulting in reduced profitability.

Strategy C: Area Diversification

Under strategy C, a trading company pursues area diversification while maintaining product and functional specialization.

Advantages. Maintaining product specialization offers the following advantages:

High Profitability. Specialization in a product segment in which the company or its country has a comparative advantage allows a trading company to be competitive in the international market and to realize relatively high profits.

Demand-Pulled Growth. By specializing in a high growth product, a trading company can expand its operations without much marketing effort.

Dealership Rights. If a trading company has ties with manufacturing firms specializing in a small number of products, it may be able to obtain exclusive dealership rights to their products.

Spillover Effect. A trading company that has exclusive rights to a brand-name product may be able to enjoy spillover effects to related product segments. Japan's Nissho-Iwai, for example, had the exclusive dealership of Nike footwear. After establishing Nike shoes in the upscale market, Nissho-Iwai was able to take advantage of Nike brand-name recognition and sell sportswear and sporting goods under the Nike brand-name.

Disadvantages. Maintaining product specialization also has significant disadvantages, including:

Volatile Demand. Earnings of a trading company that specializes in seasonal products such as clothing or construction material show wide fluctuation. Earnings volatility can also result from specialization in cyclical products. Financial performance of a company specializing in parts and machinery for oil drilling, for example, will be necessarily sensitive to business cycles in the petroleum industry.

Limited Growth Potential. As product life-cycle theory indicates, all products go through stages of introduction, growth, maturity, and eventual decline. A trading company specializing in a mature product, therefore, has limited growth potential. Of the Japanese trading companies that specialized in textile products in the pre-World-War-II era, only a handful survived and prospered through product diversification.

Overdependence on Business Groups. It has been noted that a trading company that has close ties to a business group may be able to enjoy higher profits by gaining exclusive rights to the group's products. Content with its monopoly profits, such a company may be uninterested in developing an independent marketing capability. This can lead to an overdependence on its business group, and eventually become the cause of the company's decline.

Weak Bargaining Position. A product-specialized trading company tends to have a small number of suppliers, and the loss of a single large supplier can have a major impact on the company's operations. A similar weakness exists on the demand side, where the company may be exporting to a few large buyers. Korea's Daewoo, for example, began as a textile exporter, with a significant share of its U.S. sales going to Sears Roebuck. As a result, Daewoo initially had a weak bargaining position against Sears Roebuck.

A manufacturing firm performs the marketing function by itself or delegates to traders depending on the nature of the product it handles. Especially in the following product segments, manufacturers may actually benefit from knowledge of consumer tastes and needs gained through direct marketing.[4]

1. Nonstandardized consumer goods such as clothing, where consumer tastes vary widely

2. Technology-intensive products, such as ships and automobiles, where sales often depend on demonstrated engineering competence and product knowledge

3. Products which require after-service such as television sets, refrigerators, and other consumer durables.

Large manufacturing firms generally delegate marketing responsibilities to trading companies only when they see no incremental benefit in direct marketing. Korea's virtual steel monopoly, Pohang Integrated Steel Corporation (POSCO), for example, does not export its own products. POSCO is large enough to maintain its own overseas marketing network, but has decided that it can maximize export profits by allowing several Korean GTCs to compete for its limited exportable steel supply.[5]

Evaluation. Given these disadvantages, a trading company can successfully implement strategy C as a strategy for growth only if it can satisfy certain prerequisites. The company needs close ties with manufacturing firms to ensure continued supply of its specialty products. Furthermore, the company needs to specialize in a growth product to ensure a relatively stable and buoyant demand. Strategy C would be an appropriate short-term growth strategy for a trading company established as the exporting arm of a business group. In the long-run, however, strategy C will simply suppress a trading company's growth potential. Therefore, such a company will have to examine its strategy before becoming totally dependent on the products of its business group.

Strategy D: Functional Diversification

Under strategy D, a trading company pursues functional diversification to complement its basic export function, while continuing to specialize in product and area. A trading company can potentially take on any number of functions, limited only by the ingenuity of the management. The major operating and support functions of a trading company are listed in figure 5-3.

Functional diversification is not a concept that can be unequivocally defined. This section, therefore, examines each of the various functions that a trading company can perform to evaluate the appropriateness of functional diversification as its growth strategy. Since functional specialization in exportation was assumed in the previous sections, a separate discussion on exportation is not included here.

Importation

Advantages. Functional diversification in importation has the following advantages:

Efficient Use of Overseas Branch Network. Importation, like exportation, links domestic and foreign economies through the movement of tangible goods. A trading company, therefore, may be able to use its overseas branch network, initially established to facilitate exports, to engage in importation, thereby benefiting from the synergy effects of diversification without significant additional cost. A company engaging in both import and export is likely to be more cost-effective than two separate companies, each devoted exclusively to import or export.

Access to Manufacturers. Importing raw materials for a manufacturing firm enables a trading company to develop a close working relationship with that manufacturing firm. If the trading company has a monopoly on certain raw-material imports, it can use this leverage to gain export rights to the manufacturer's products.

Countertrade Capability. Since the early 1980s, countertrade has played an increasingly important role in the international movement of tangible goods.[6] Countertrade became popular among countries with chronic trade deficits as

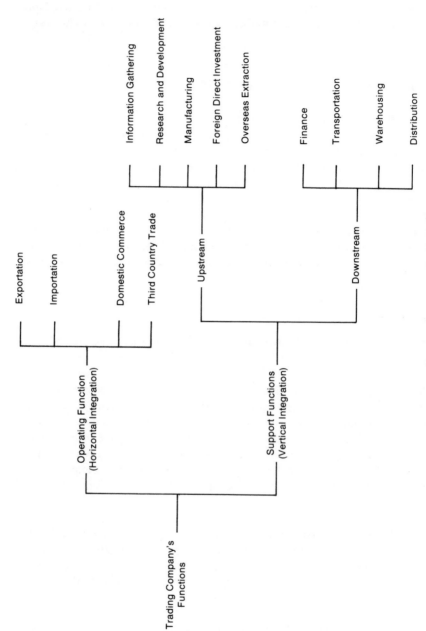

Figure 5-3. Functions of the Trading Company

a means of reducing the deficit by paying for imports directly with domestic products. Much of the world's countertrade originated in the Soviet Union and East European countries, but soon spread to OPEC member states, China, Mexico, and Brazil. Recently, developed countries, especially Canada, Sweden, Switzerland, and Japan, have begun to participate actively.

For example, Iran made a contract to import $200 million mutton from New Zealand and export the same value of crude oil as a way of payment. Poland made a proposal to import electronic products from General Electric on the condition that GE purchase Poland-made ham and cheese. To cope with such countertrade practices, GE had already established General Electric Trading Company, as was described in detail in chapter 4. As another example, Libya demanded that Daewoo Corporation of Korea receive crude oil as a payment for the latter's construction service there. The Philippines demanded that another GTC in Korea buy its bananas in return for importing Korean fertilizers. Taiwan also suggested an exchange of bananas for Korean pears. Latin American countries like Equador, Mexico, and Argentina have offered to trade their crude oil or beef for Japanese fire-engines or steel products.

Under these circumstances, in the United States, Korea, Japan, and all over the world, it is imperative for a trading firm to strengthen its import function to complement its export activity in global markets.

Disadvantages. However, importation, which is not like exportation, has the following disadvantages in strengthening its functions.

The Need for Highly Professional Ability. Because importation parallels exportation, only going in a different direction, one may be misled to think that similar professional ability is required for importation and exportation. However, importation requires higher professional ability and skills. Unlike exportation, where exporters can carry out negotiations with knowledge of cost data on export products, importation is made with a limited number of trade partners and without cost data on imported products, thus it is harder for importers to ascertain if the deal made with exporters is truly the best or not.

For example, an exporter selling a $3 shirt for $4 knows that he has made a profitable sale, although the margin may be less than he hoped for. An importer, however, needs a higher level of market knowledge. Consider an importer waiting to buy a VLCC load of crude oil amounting to 1.8 million barrels at the Rotterdam spot market. On the first day, the spot price was at $15 per barrel. On the second day, it fell to $14.75. On the third day, when the price fell to $14.50 per barrel, the company decided to buy the 1.8 million barrels of oil that it needed, convinced that the spot price had hit the bottom for the foreseeable future. On the fourth day, after the company signed a contract to buy 1.8 million barrels at $14.50, the spot priced dropped to $14.25. Had the company correctly projected the spot price, it would have saved $450,000 by waiting just one more day; the company, in effect, loss $450,000 in potential profit.

Impact on Manufacturers' Profitability. The cost of raw material or component imports can directly affect manufacturers' production costs. Manufacturing firms in resource-poor countries generally have a high import content, and hence are particularly sensitive to variations in raw-material import costs. As a result, manufacturing firms often prefer to import raw materials directly to control their prices. This is true even for a manufacturing firm in a business group with its own trading company. Therefore it is more difficult to consolidate import activities of group companies in a trading company than to consolidate export activities.

Limited Usefulness of Branch Network. Many manufacturing firms see little benefit in consolidating in a trading company both import and export functions. Exportation depends on access to large number of buyers, which a trading company can effectively provide. In the case of importation, however, manufacturers often prefer to develop reliable supply lines with a small number of well-established foreign producers. Furthermore, the number of potential suppliers for many raw material imports, such as rubber, raw sugar, and petroleum, are limited. Therefore, a large number of manufacturers need to establish a working relationship with only a small number of foreign suppliers, and a large overseas branch network constitutes an unnecessary overhead expense.

Evaluation. As indicated, importation is a business requiring a high level of expertise. A trading company that has specialized in exportation cannot hope to become a viable importer by simply undertaking this additional function. Furthermore, manufacturing firms may be reluctant to delegate import responsibilities to trading companies.

For a trading company, the benefit of diversifying into importation is nevertheless clear: it affords an opportunity for increased sales and profits. Manufacturing firms that rely on a small number of foreign suppliers run the risk of becoming their captive market. In the long run, therefore, reliability of supply may not justify potentially excessive import costs. This is particularly true as local trading companies develop expertise in importation, thereby assuring relatively stable supplies at competitive prices. Certainly, from the national perspective, it is to a country's advantage to have locally owned trading companies shop around for low-cost foreign suppliers.

The question, therefore, is not so much whether a trading company should diversify into importation but how it can effectively develop this import function. Two major methods can be considered. First, import function of manufacturers must be consolidated into trading companies. This is not a strategic move that a trading company can necessarily undertake for itself, since manufacturing firms are the ones to make the decision. The task is easier for a trading company that belongs to a business group. It is the responsibility of the chief executive of the holding company or the whole group to recognize the benefits of a consolidated import function and to have the trading company purchase the whole group's import requirements. From the perspective of an individual manufacturing unit, delegating raw-material import rights may constitute a source of inefficiency, but for the group as a whole, the buying power of a large-scale importer can reduce overall import costs.

Second, a trading company must train specialists. Participation in the futures market, such as the London Metal Exchange or Chicago Board of Trade, requires specialists with years of experience. Therefore, a trading company should be prepared to make long-term investments in human-resources development before it can become an efficient importer.

Domestic Commerce

Advantages. Functional diversification in domestic commerce has the following advantages:

Growth Potential. Participation in domestic commerce contributes directly to the sales and profits of a trading company. In the case of the nine Japanese *sogo-shosha*, for example, domestic sales accounted for about 50 percent of their annual total. Furthermore, experience in domestic commerce can lead to increased exports through shared marketing expertise.

Basis for Stability. Domestic commerce can provide stability for a trading company heavily dependent on the international market. The domestic market is usually less volatile, and a company's involvement in the market makes business operations less cyclical.

Utilization of Marketing Capabilities. Except for subtle changes in method to account for cultural differences, the basic skills of marketing are required for effective penetration of markets everywhere. A trading company that has developed successful domestic marketing skills may be able to transfer them to foreign markets.

Test Marketing. Less-developed countries generally enter the international trade arena by exporting commodities or labor-intensive goods. As wages increase, however, a country exporting labor-intensive products will begin to lose its comparative advantage in the original product segment, and will be forced to export more expensive, higher value-added products. These new products, however, will not be available for exportation until their quality improves through trials and errors in the domestic market. Thus the domestic market can serve as a test market for products before they are exported. Consider the case of Korea's Lucky-Goldstar International. The company's operations in the clothing industry began with the domestic distribution of ready-made clothes under the brand-name Bando Fashion, and launched an exporting business after establishing domestic consumer acceptance. Then certain specific consumer demands abroad led to subsequent improvements in the quality and styling of Bando Fashion, so that domestic and foreign experiences effectively reinforced each other.

Disadvantages. Some of the disadvantages of functional diversification in domestic commerce include:

High Level of Competition. Domestic markets tend to be highly competitive, with many small participants. A trading company that tries to diversify into domestic commerce may face not only fierce competition from established participants attempting to protect their market position, but also criticisms from the government and the public intent on protecting small- to medium-sized businesses.

Limited Growth Potential. Domestic markets are by definition smaller than the international market, and in many countries, segments of the domestic market can be easily dominated by one large company. Domestic markets, therefore, promise a rather limited growth potential, unless the economy as a whole is growing rapidly. A trading company hoping particularly to realize economies of scale will not show much interest in domestic commerce.

Small Market Size. In many product segments, the domestic market may be simply too small for a trading company to operate profitably. If a product is new, the market may not yet have been formed; if a product is maturing, the market may be shrinking.

Evaluation. Managers of trading companies in small countries often dismiss domestic commerce as irrelevant because of its small size. In contrast, the international arena offers a limitless opportunity for growth. However, participation in domestic commerce has several advantages. Most important, it provides an element of stability to a trading company's overall operation. As long as the worldwide economy is growing, a trading company will not be compelled to take part in domestic commerce, which seems to offer only fierce competition and limited growth potential. In a worldwide recession, however, heavy dependence on international trade can lead to rapidly deteriorating profitability.

Unless a trading company operates with government assurance that it will be saved from financial difficulties, it cannot automatically subordinate stability to growth as a corporate objective. Therefore, it needs to balance its participation in both the high-growth but volatile international market and the low-growth but more predictable domestic market.

Third-Country Trade

Advantage: Unlimited Growth Potential. Third-country trade is not limited by the resources of any particular country.[7] In third-country trade, a trading company finds and matches both the buyer and seller abroad through its overseas market-information capabilities. Third-country trade, therefore, potentially offers the opportuntity for limitless growth.

Disadvantages. The disadvantages of diversification into third-country trade include the following:

High Level of Expertise. Third-country trade is more than concurrent participation in import and export, and requires a higher level of expertise than either of these two traditional trade activities. In third-country trade, neither the buyer nor the seller is the trading company's home country. Therefore, participation in third-country trade requires a comprehensive market knowledge of many foreign countries.

High Risk. In third-country trade, a trading company has no source of comparative advantage other than its reputation and ability to buy and sell products across national boundaries. This inherently involves a high level of risk.

Evaluation. Many trading companies participate in third-country trade of certain specialized products. Phibro is one of the largest of such companies, with an annual trading volume of over $20 billion. A subsidiary of Phibro-Salomon, it trades primarily in nonmetallic and organic minerals, crude oil, sugar, and agricultural commodities. Another notable company is Marc Rich & Co. Established in 1974 by Marc Rich, a former senior trader at Phibro, it has grown into one of the largest crude oil trading companies in the world. In spite of its recent tax complications, the meteoric success of Marc Rich & Co. is a testimony to the importance of professional expertise in third-country trade.

Because of the high level of expertise required, a trading company can only gradually develop a third-country trade function. As increasingly large numbers of its employees are transferred from one foreign country to another, taking with them market knowledge acquired in the previous assignment, a trading company will begin to accumulate the comprehensive market knowledge required. Expertise grows naturally out of continued expansion of export and import capabilities.

Information Gathering

Advantages. Diversification into information gathering has the following advantages:

Source of Value-Added. A trading company links a producer and a consumer by filling the information gap between them. This is its fundamental source of value-added.

Increased Use of Branch Network. Rather than using overseas branch offices simply as outlets for its exports, a trading company can use them to gather local market information.

Development of Information Industry. Overseas market information is a valuable commodity. In an increasingly uncertain international economic environment, a trading company can gather information both for internal use and for sale to unrelated parties.

Disadvantages. The disadvantages of diversification into information gathering include:

Uncertain Investment Value. Unlike fixed-asset investments, investments in information-gathering capability cannot be easily evaluated. Some managers may be reluctant to invest in a function which results in little immediate and generally intangible reward.

Difficulty in Maintaining Resources. Developing information-gathering capability requires an investment in human resources, such as training of market analysts. A departure of these human resources constitutes a lost investment and a lost information-gathering ability of the company.

Evaluation. Market information is the fundamental source of value-added for a trading company. Information gathering is as basic as exportation, and should be developed even before functional diversification into importation, domestic commerce, third-country trade, and certainly other support activities can be seriously considered.

Research and Development

Unlike a manufacturing firm, a trading company does not have the independent ability to develop a new technology or product. Therefore, a trading company's functional diversification into research and development represents financial investments in a new venture company with a viable idea and technology but without the capital resources to actually produce its innovation.

Japanese *sogo-shosha* have recently taken increasing interest in research and development. The new industry segments in which they are actively participating are robotics, electronics, semiconductors, deep sea-bed mining, alternate energy, and genetic engineering.

Advantage: Exclusive Right to Trade. If a new product is successfully developed, the investor trading company will acquire an exclusive right to distribute that product, resulting in monopoly profits.

Disadvantages. Diversification into research and development can have the following disadvantages:

Large Investment. The investment required, especially in electronics and alternate energy fields, can reach into hundreds of millions of dollars. A trading company may need to provide only a small portion of the total investment to gain the distribution rights. Nevertheless, the investment represents a major demand on a trading company's limited financial resources. Generally not involved in manufacturing, a trading company has limited depreciation allowance, and profit margins tend to be as low as the 0.1-0.5 percent range. A trading company is therefore unlikely to be able to make significant discretionary expenditures on research and development without limiting expenditures elsewhere.

High Risk. There is no guarantee that an investment will result in the development of a commercially viable product. Having low working capital, a trading company is particularly ill-suited to invest in new high-risk ventures, where return on investment is not at all assured.

Choice of Venture. New ventures tend to require an extremely high level of technology, and an investment decision is the result of an evaluation of the commercial viability of that technology. Trading companies, unlike venture capitalists for example, generally lack the technological competence or familiarity with the participants in the high tech field to judge effectively the feasibility of a proposed project.

Evaluation. Given these major concerns, it is not at all clear that functional diversification into research and development should be pursued. For small and unsophisticated trading companies, certainly, research and development poses an insurmountable drain of financial resources.

Manufacturing

Advantages. The advantages of diversification into manufacturing include the following:

Higher Value-Added. By developing its own manufacturing capability, a trading company can increase its value-added. Furthermore, if production is sufficient to meet only demand during the low season or business cycle, and any excess demand is contracted out to other manufacturers, diversification into manufacturing can stabilize a trading company's earnings.

Better Quality Control. With its own manufacturing facility, a trading company can control quality to cater to consumers' particular demands and expectations. It can therefore experience a lower rate of returned goods.

Disadvantages. Two disadvantages of diversification into manufacturing are:

High Fixed-Asset Investment. Manufacturing requires considerable fixed-asset investment. Given a trading company's low working-capital position, diversification into manufacturing may jeopardize financial flexibility.

Reduced Competitiveness. Manufacturing subsidiaries of big trading companies generally have to pay a higher level of wages than independent manufacturers, even for unskilled workers. This tends to reduce the price-competitiveness of a trading company's manufacturing operations.

Evaluation. Diversification into manufacturing offers the prospects of increased profitability in the short run. In the long run, however, a trading company may prove to be a high-cost manufacturer, and its production facilities may become a continual limitation on its financial resources. Especially in the case of a trading company belonging to a business group, manufacturing responsibilities are better delegated to other related subsidiaries, if necessary by incorporating a new business entity. In this way the trading company will still be able to enjoy higher earnings by handling a wide range of products without diversifying into a function that it is financially ill-equipped to handle.

Foreign Direct Investment

Foreign direct investment increases with the growing protectionism among major import countries. There are two major forms of foreign direct investments designed to elude the impact of trade barriers: local investments and third-country investments. In a local investment, a foreign company establishes a subsidiary directly in the major import country. Such subsidiaries usually assemble the final product with imported complete-knock-down or semi-knock-down components. In third-country investment, a foreign company sets up operations in a third country where labor costs are lower than in its own country, and where exports are not restricted by the major import country.

Advantage: Alternative to Exportation. Given the increasing trend toward protectionism worldwide, foreign direct investment can effectively substitute for or complement potential reductions in export earnings. By participating in the local economy through foreign direct investment, a trading company may also alleviate criticisms against large exporters from the host-country government and the public.

Disadvantages. Some disadvantages of foreign direct investment are:

Investment Financing. Foreign direct investment requires substantial and long-term equity financing.

Management Difficulties. Foreign direct investment requires a trading company to set up a manufacturing operation in an alien business environment, where unfamiliarity with local language, habits, laws, and regulations can cause difficulties in day-to-day management.

Evaluation. Trading companies, as much as other business entities, should be familiar with the problems of operating in a foreign environment. Therefore, foreign direct investment can be considered an effective method of penetrating an overseas market that resists imports from overseas.

Overseas Raw-Material Extraction

Just as foreign direct investment can complement exports, overseas raw material extraction can complement imports. Figure 5-4 shows the various methods that a trading company can use to diversify into overseas extraction.

Advantage: Import Rights. In overseas extraction, a trading company's primary objective is not to become a profitable extraction company, but to

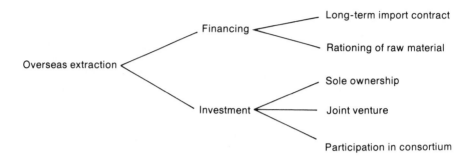

Figure 5-4. Methods for Overseas Raw-Material Extraction

gain import rights to the extracted raw materials. Therefore, it is to the advantage of a trading company to make the smallest amount of investment possible to gain the distribution rights. This can be best accomplished by financing an extraction operation in return for a long-term import contract.

Disadvantages. Disadvantages of diversification into overseas raw-material extraction include the following:

Long Waiting Period. Raw-material extraction requires a lengthy period of exploration and preparation. Preparation can take several years for oil drilling and metal-ore mining.

Large Investment. Extraction requires a large initial investment and continuous financing until actual production begins. Especially when local financing is not available, an extraction project can tie up large sums of capital that could have been used elsewhere.

High Risk. Any new venture involves a variety of risks. For raw-material extraction, uncertainty over location, despite sophisticated geological surveys, and the high level of capital involved add elements of risk.

Resource Nationalism. Since 1973, when OPEC successfully demonstrated the economic power of raw-material producers, there has been a trend toward resource nationalism. Host countries have begun to demand larger shares from successful raw-material extraction, and in some cases, have demanded outright nationalization. Furthermore, host countries have begun to demand increased local processing of raw materials before exportation.

Evaluation. If it succeeds, raw-material extraction can be a highly rewarding business for a trading company. However, the need for raw materials fluctuates widely according to final consumer demand. Given the extent of the uncertainty involved on both the demand and the supply side, diversification into extraction appears to be a high-risk, high-return strategy.

Finance

Trading companies can diversify into finance by becoming owners of financial institutions, including commercial banks, brokerage houses, or insurance companies, as in Korea. Conversely, a financial institution can invest in a trading company, as in the United States, combined with interlocking directorship, as in Japan. The issue is not so much what kind of a relationship a trading company establishes with a financial institution, but the nature of special financing that the trader can receive compared to other business entities. Privileged financing can take the form of lower interest on loans or access to higher levels of debt financing than other business entities are granted.

Advantage: Increased Financial Flexibility. Close ties with financial institutions can greatly increase the financial flexibility of a trading company, thereby providing competitive advantage against other companies without such ties.

Disadvantage: Government Regulation. In some countries, the government strictly and systematically regulates interest on loans and the level of bank exposures. In such economies, a close relationship with a financial institution does not provide any particular competitive edge.

Evaluation. The importance of close ties to financial institutions is demonstrated by the Japanese *sogo-shosha*, which receive both lower priced loans and higher exposure limits from their banks compared to other business entities. Both Taiwan and the United States saw the value of such financial support, and made commercial banks key players in the establishment of large trading companies and export trading companies. Even in a country with strict banking regulations, maintaining close ties with financial institutions will prove valuable as the latter may be able to exercise some covert flexibility in their lending policies.

Other Support Functions

Insurance, transportation, and warehousing are some of the other major functions generally contracted out by trading companies. As its volume increases, a trading company should to able to internalize these functions for increased value-added. Such functions are generally hidden behind the primary transactions resulting from a trading company's operating functions in exportation, importation, domestic commerce, or third-country trade. Charges for such support functions often go without much negotiation, and therefore, can lead to deceptively high profits.[8] Strengthening mundane support functions can increase a trading company's profitability just as effectively as diversification into risky fields like research and development or raw-material extraction.

Functional Diversification Summarized

The preceding evaluations of a trading company's various functions are summarized in table 5-1. Among the operating functions, diversification into

Table 5-1
Functional Diversification Summarized

Function	Advantages	Disadvantages	Evaluation
Importation	Efficient use of overseas branch network Provides access to manufacturers Countertrade capability	High level of expertise Impacts manufacturers' profitability Limited use of branch network	Pursue
Domestic commerce	Growth potential Foundation for stability Utilization of marketing capabilities Test marketing	High level of competition Limited growth potential Small market size	Pursue
Third-country trade	Unlimited growth potential	High level of expertise High risk	Develop with time
Information gathering	Source of value-added Increased use of overseas branch network Development of information industry	Uncertain investment value Difficulty to maintain resources	Pursue
Research and development	Monopolistic right to trade	Large investment High risk Uncertain choice of venture	Inappropriate
Manufacturing	High value-added Better quality control	High fixed-asset investment Reduced competitiveness	Only in the long-run
Foreign direct investment	Alternative to exportation	High financing requirement Management difficulties	Pursue only where necessary
Overseas extraction	Import rights	Long waiting period Large investment High risk Resource nationalism	Pursue very selectively
Finance	Increased financial flexibility	Government regulation	Pursue
Other support	High profitability	High expertise required	Pursue selectively

importation and domestic commerce should be aggressively pursued. Among the support functions, information gathering and finance can give a competitive edge. A trading company should be a bit more cautious in venturing into third-country trade, foreign direct investment, or support functions such as insurance, transportation, and warehousing. A trading company may not necessarily have the economies of scale necessary to enjoy the benefits of such diversification. In contrast, research and development, overseas extraction, and manufacturing all demand a great deal of financial resources, and need to be very cautiously approached.

Strategy D, functional diversification, suggests that a trading company can concurrently diversify into operating and support functions. Conceptually, this is correct. From the Japanese experience, however, it is apparent that a trading company is more easily able to diversify into the less sophisticated operating functions, and slowly acquires support functions as it grows in size and gains higher levels of expertise in the international market.

Strategy E: Product and Area Diversification

Under strategy E, a trading company pursues product and area diversification, while continuing to emphasize exportation.

Advantages. The advantages of product and area diversification include the following:

Government Support. Under strategy E, a trading company can rapidly increase its export amount. Therefore, in a country where export expansion has been adopted as the national economic policy, such a trading company can maintain cordial relations with the government and gain visible as well as invisible favors.

Improved Company Image. Due to the nature of trading, the general public evaluates a trading company's performance more often by its export amount than by its profits or stock price. A rapid increase in exports under strategy D, therefore, can improve a company's image and reputation. In some cases, a higher reputation will even allow the company to attract more easily capable new employees.

Increased Access to Financing. Governments often provide subsidies, including trade financing, to exporters. Such government support is seldom available in importation, third-country trade, or domestic commerce. A trading company emphasizing exportation, therefore, is likely to enjoy a higher cash flow.

Economies of Scale. As export volume increases rapidly, the burden of fixed cost will generally fall, and marginal profitability will increase.

Future Profit. With rapid increases in export, a trading company will quickly move up the learning curve. Higher volume, therefore, leads to higher profitability in the future.

Disadvantages. Some disadvantages to diversification in product and area include:

Unprofitable Segments. Under strategy E, a trading company may diversify into new products and areas without carefully considering the potential profit. As the number of segments increases, there will inevitably be segments in which the company takes a loss.

Lack of Expertise. Under strategy E, a trading company is less likely to make the effort to develop expertise in any particular segment. Profitability, therefore, may suffer as a result of a lack of sales engineers or area specialists.

Evaluation. Strategy E offers the potential for overall profits in the future in return for the probability of lower profits in each of the segments at the present. Further elaboration, however, is needed before the strategy's merit can be evaluated.

Strategy E seems to suggest that product and area diversification should be pursued concurrently and resources divided equally. In practice, however, it is necessary to establish priorities. The decision of whether to pursue product or area diversification first is a critical step in implementing a strategy for growth. As shown in figure 5-5, a previously specialized company can choose to develop either new products (1 → 2) or new markets (1 → 3). The choice

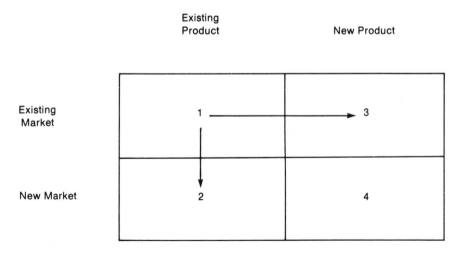

Figure 5-5. Strategy for Product and Area Diversification

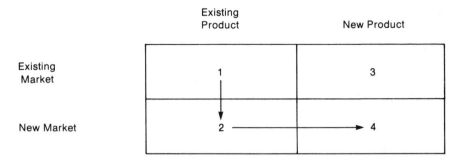

Figure 5-6. Modified Strategy for Product and Area Diversification

is not obvious. By considering the experience of the Korean GTCs, we can gain some insight into this problem.

Korean GTCs were established as the trading arms of large enterprise groups. By the time the government established the ordinance to create the GTC in 1975, Korean business groups already had some international exposure but in a limited number of product segments. When government requisites for GTC designation demanded both product and area diversification, the companies reacted by merging and acquiring existing manufacturing firms. The merger and acquisition program, however, did not necessarily provide exportable goods.

The new-product blocks in figure 5-5 refer to the development of exportable goods. Merger and acquisition of manufacturing firms by Korean GTCs provided domestically saleable products, but not necessarily exportable goods. Korean GTCs, in fact, found it easier to sell their traditional products in new markets than to develop new products for traditional markets. Based on the Korean experience, figure 5-5 can be modified as shown in figure 5-6 to show that it is easier to develop new markets (1 → 2), and then diversify into new export products (2 → 4).

Therefore, a trading company can successfully adopt strategy E for growth by initially pursuing area diversification, thus assuring relatively stable profits based on exports of traditional products with proven international competitiveness. Subsequently, the company can pursue product diversification as a long-term strategy for growth.

Strategy F: Product and Functional Diversification

Under strategy F, a trading company maintains area specialization, but diversifies into new products and functions. Strategy F, comparable to past growth strategies of European trading houses, offers a limited growth potential. Unlike early European trading houses, a present-day trading company cannot hope to benefit from the political influence of its country in certain overseas regions. Furthermore, as noted in the discussion of strategy B, a trading company can at the most dominate relatively small economies, which often have unstable political environments.

By concentrating its resources, a trading company can establish a transient dominance over a foreign market. Korean companies, for example, dominated the construction market in Saudi Arabia, Nigeria, and Libya immediately following the oil crisis. Economic power in a foreign country unaccompanied by political influence, however, can evaporate quickly, as the subsequent erosion of Korean companies' construction market share in the Middle East demonstrates. Concentration of resources in one area can expose a trading company to an extremely high level of country risk. Strategy F offers the lure of rapid growth in the short run, but is an inappropriate long-term growth strategy for a trading company.

Strategy G: Area and Functional Diversification

Under strategy G, a trading company pursues area and functional diversification while maintaining product specialization. In practice, strategy G describes a company that has pursued area diversification under strategy C, taking on new functions to complement its export operations.

The discussion of strategy C indentified the major shortcomings of an area-diversification strategy as volatile demand, limited growth potential, overdependence on business groups, and weak bargaining position due to undivided marketing responsibilities between a trading company and a manufacturing firm. If functional diversification mitigates some of these concerns, strategy C must be considered a more effective strategy for growth.

Advantages. Some of the advantages of combining area and functional diversification include:

Counterbalance Volatile Demand. In the discussion of strategy C, seasonal and cyclical demands were identified as two major sources of earnings volatility. Seasonality tends to be predictable and therefore relatively easy to counteract. Clothing exporters to the United States, for example, quickly learn that demand is highest during the two to three months before Christmas, and that the production of winter clothes must begin in spring and shipping be completed by the end of summer. With experience and early planning, a trading company can easily project and prepare for seasonal variations in demand.

Unlike seasonality, cyclical demand has no particular pattern. Business cycles can be induced by many external pressures, from wars to fuel shortages. An extensive information-gathering network, however, can serve as an early warning system, thus alleviating the impact of an economic downturn. Companies like Phibro and Marc Rich & Co., for example, maintain extensive intelligence networks spanning the oil-producing countries, oil companies, and major consumer countries, which allow them to monitor closely changes in market condition and to react more rapidly than other firms.

Competitive Edge over Manufacturers. As noted, a manufacturing firm that has the ability to undertake overseas marketing independently will delegate that responsibility to a trading company only if it sees incremental benefit. A trading company may be able to provide higher volume or lower export expense. The benefit to a manufacturing firm is increased if the trading company can also provide support functions such as transportation, warehousing, customs-clearance services, and insurance. Functional diversification into such trade-related services can increase the trading company's chances of gaining marketing rights from a manufacturing firm. In the early 1960s, when Japanese manufacturers began to export independently, *sogo-shosha* sought to improve their bargaining position against the manufacturers by diversifying into transportation, customs-clearance services, warehousing, and other trade support activities.

Disadvantage: Limited Growth Potential. A trading company specializing in a mature product faces limited growth potential. Such a company can independently attempt to lengthen the remaining useful life of its product or develop a follow-on product by investing in research and development. A trading company is, however, ill-equipped to undertake product development; it lacks the financial resources, the technological know-how, and the manufacturing capability to support such a project.

Generally without manufacturing facilities, a trading company has little or no fixed-asset investment tied to a specific product segment. When a product matures, a trading company can withdraw from that segment with relative ease. Rather than diversifying into research and development, a trading company should move into a new product segment when its traditional product shows signs of maturity.

Evaluation. In some cases, functional diversification can effectively compensate for the shortcomings of product specialization. Extensive information-gathering capabilities can mitigate the effects of business cycles. Further, diversification into trade-related functions allows a trading company to improve its competitive position against manufacturing firms.

While functional diversification can effectively complement area diversification as a strategy for growth, there is no compelling reason for a trading company capable of functional diversification to stop short of product diversification. A company that can offer various trade services in one product segment can often transfer those capabilities to other segments without much difficulty. A trading company that transports clothing for one client in a country based on its extensive functional services can just as easily transport footwear for another in the same country. Strategy G, therefore, should be considered a valuable but transient growth strategy toward complete diversification.

Strategy H: Complete Diversification

Under strategy H, a trading company pursues diversification in product, area, and function. Chapter 2 showed that among the present-day trading companies Japanese *sogo-shosha* have most successfully followed this strategy.

Advantages. The advantages of complete diversification include:

Economies of Scale. Trading companies that are diversified by product and area have already achieved fairly high economies of scale, and therefore find functional diversification much easier than would a small trading company. A company that has an annual trade volume of 100 million tons can enter the shipping industry just by catering its own transportation needs.

Competitive Position against Manufacturers. A manufacturing firm can achieve extensive area and functional diversification with relative ease. It is more difficult to divide manufacturing capabilities between a large number of products. Further, a manufacturing firm is ill-equipped to participate in increasingly important countertrade. A trading company's ability to handle a wide range of products, therefore, gives it a competitive edge over manufacturing firms.

Flexibility in Management. With its extensive information-gathering capability, a trading company has a considerable ability to evaluate the profitability and growth potentials of various products in various markets. Unconstrained by high barriers to withdrawal resulting from heavy fixed-asset investments, trading company management has flexibility to redeploy its resources from one segment to another.

Disadvantages. As noted in the discussion of strategy D, selective functional diversification is a valuable growth strategy. An overly ambitious diversification program, however, can be self-defeating, bringing the following disadvantages:

Limited Available Resources. Even a large trading company has limited human and capital resources. Further diversification must compete with working-capital requirements in existing operations.

External Complexities. As a trading company becomes increasingly diversified, it must operate in a larger number of foreign business environments. Therefore, it must compete with local companies in an increased number of countries and establish relations with an increased number of governments.

Lower Efficiency. Diversification in product, area, and function without a focus can simply divide a company's resources, and lead to a greater chance of inefficiency in each segment. Therefore, only a large-scale trading company will be able to pursue complete diversification without significantly sacrificing its efficiency and eventual profitability.

Need for Horizontal Cooperation. Complete diversification can result in many units, each operating to reach only its designated responsibility and individual profit goals. If a trading company is to avoid such fragmentation, it will have to institute high levels of horizontal cooperation and coordination among its numerous units.

Evaluation. The value of synergy effects resulting from complete diversification has already been considered in chapter 2. It is clear from the preceding discussions on the advantages of complete diversification that strategy H is a desirable long-term growth strategy. It is also clear, however, that the strategy can be valuable only for a trading company of considerable size, since efforts at complete diversification make great demands on a company's limited resources.

It is not possible to state absolutely the critical size that makes complete diversification a wise strategy for growth. A comparison of the sizes of Japanese *sogo-shosha*, which pursue complete diversification, and Korean GTCs, which are diversified only in product and area, does provide a sense of the scale involved. Based on 1983 data, the average paid-in-capital of Korean GTCs was roughly one-fifth the average paid-in-capital of Japanese *sogo-shosha*. Korean GTCs had one-twentieth the total assets and total sales, one-fifth the exports, and one-third the number of overseas branch offices as Japanese *sogo-shosha* had.

Size is certainly not the only criterion for complete diversification. Many other factors, from management attitude and ability to lack of exportable products and an underdeveloped services sector in its country, can affect a trading company's ability to successfully pursue strategy H.

Process of Strategy Implementation

The strengths and weaknessess of the eight generic strategies for growth are summarized in table 5-2. These strategies can be reexamined, in three groups.

Table 5-2
Eight Generic Strategies Summarized

Strategy	Advantages	Disadvantages	Evaluation
A: Complete specialization	Increased efficiency	Proportionally high fixed costs Foregone growth potential	Trade-off between volume and profit
B: Product diversification	Country representation Increased value-added Competitive edge over manufacturers	Small market size Limited growth potential High future uncertainties High country risk	Use of a company's relative strength
C: Area diversification	Based on internationally competitive product Demand-pulled growth Dealership rights Spill-over effect	Volatile demand Limited growth potential Overdependence on enterprise groups Weak bargaining position	Strong initial strategy
D: Functional diversification	Complements exportation Source of competitive edge High profitability	High expertise required	Appropriate growth strategy
E: Product and area diversification	Government support Improved image Increased financial access Economies of scale High future profit potential	Unprofitable segments Lack of expertise	High trade-off
F: Product and functional diversification	Market monopoly	Limited growth potential	Inappropriate growth strategy
G: Area and functional diversification	Counterbalance with volatile demand Competitive edge over manufacturers	Limited growth potential	Intermediate step from C to H
H: Complete diversification	Economies of scale Competitive edge over manufacturers Management flexibility	Limited available resources External complexities Lower efficiency Horizontal cooperation needed	Long-term growth strategy

Gradual Move Toward Complete Diversification

Beginning with area diversification (strategy C), a trading company can gradually develop into a general trading company. After achieving area diversification, the company can diversify into new functions (strategy G). Once area and functional diversification are established, the company can begin to pursue complete diversification (strategy H).[9]

This stepped growth model, C → G → H, differs from past experiences. Korean GTCs have already achieved product and area diversification, and are at the initial stages of integrating new functional capabilities. Similarly, Japanese *sogo-shosha* began to achieve functional diversification only in the

1950s, after establishing product and area diversification. In both cases, the course was C → E → H.

Under strategy E, product and area diversification, there is a tendency to sacrifice profitability in return for higher volume. In contrast, under strategy G, area and functional diversification, a trading company can maintain its profitability by acquiring support functions, while continuing to trade its traditional product with proven international competitiveness. The proposed model C → G → H, therefore, permits a trading company to move toward complete diversification without experiencing the pains of reduced profitability.

Specialization

A trading company that continues to pursue product diversification (strategy B) will become an area-specific trader. Similarly, a company that continues to pursue functional diversification (strategy D) will become a function-specific trader.

However, it is not likely that a company can concurrently pursue both product and area diversification (strategy F). The market size in a specialized area may be too small for functional diversification, and if it is not, the company may be able to maintain market dominance in its product segments because of a high level of local competition. Therefore, strategy F is not considered a viable long-term strategy for growth.

Pursuit of Profitability

Experiences in Japan and Korea show that a trading company can be easily lured into pursuing product and area diversification (strategy E) as the strategy for growth. Strategy E, however, often results in increased volume without the benefit of increased profits. Concerned with deteriorating profitability, such a company may decide to forego any further efforts at diversification and again adopt strategy A toward selective specialization, driven solely by profitability criterion.

Long-term Implications for Volume versus Profit

As shown in chapter 4, trading companies are established in many countries as a part of the government's export expansion program, and government requisites and public pressure demand that these companies achieve high export volume. While apparently successful on the surface, the actual profitability of such operations tends to suffer rapidly, and the companies are forced to seek improved profits.

Under this circumstance, the choice between volume and profit is an immediate policy problem forced upon trading company managers. Consider a trading company that can sell steel abroad at a price only equal to or lower than its own purchase price from a monopolistic steel manufacturer. The company can increase its volume only at the expense of a financial loss or, at best, zero profit. From a short-term perspective, the decision to undertake this unprofitable steel export is clearly absurd.

The issue is less clear from a long-term perspective. In a competitive market, continued growth leads to increased profits in the long run. This position is supported by both management theory and empirical evidence.[10] Furthermore, for a trading company that relies on economies of scale as the source of its competitive advantage, continued growth is particularly important. A trading company, therefore, should take a long-term perspective and pursue higher volume in spite of potential low profits in the short run.

A trading company should choose the viability of a potential transaction not solely on the basis of immedite profitability, but also for its long-term benefits. A transaction does not have to result in immediate income to benefit a trading company's operations. Some other potential benefits that can compensate for low profitability are:

1. Source of profit
2. Creates business opportunities in operating functions
3. Creates business opportunities in support functions
4. Provides experience
5. Leads to improved company image
6. Preempts competition
7. Establishes a basis in a new market
8. Serves as a stepping stone to other opportunities

Denial of long-term growth potential is not the only shortcoming in an attempt to return to selective specializaiton. It is one thing for a small trading company to forego opportunities for rapid growth and to maintain specialization for high profitability. Yet, it is another matter for an established large-scale trading company to shrink its operations and return to selective specialization. Public image is more than a simple psychological reward, and hence loss of image through reduction of size will give a negative impact on the company's actual operation. A smaller company will also have a more limited access to the financial markets, and its financial flexibility and cash flow will be significantly reduced. Furthermore, it will have a difficult time establishing its credibility, both at home and abroad.

There are other factors, both visible and invisible, that can influence the choice of strategy objective between profitability and growth. It is not an area where theory can necessarily provide a useful solution. Choosing is an art, based on the evaluation of circumstances often beyond management's immediate control.

Notes

1. The reader will note the difference in the use of the hexahedron in this chapter and in chapter 2. In chapter 2, the hexahedron was used to represent the present diversification mode of the four international business forms. In this chapter, it is used to identify the diversification strategies available to a trading company as strategies for growth.

2. Michel E. Porter, *Competitive Strategy*, The Free Press, 1980, p. 22.

3. *Goldstar Co. Ltd.*, HBS Case Services (0-385-264), Harvard Business School, Boston.

4. In Japan, for example, most automobile and consumer electronics manufacturers export directly. *Sogo-shosha*'s strength continues to be in product segments that require little sales engineering, such as plywood, food, steel, textile and chemicals.

5. Until the late 1970s, POSCO directly exported its own products.

6. In traditional barter trade, one product is exchanged directly for another product with an equivalent value. Countertrade, in contrast, settles each transaction with a monetary payment. However, for every import, there is a corresponding export that is to be settled within a specified time period. Countertrade is in effect barter trade with a time lag.

7. Third-country trade is part of merchandizing trade. The term is not strictly accurate. There are not three countries involved, but two countries and a trading company from an unrelated third country. Third-country trade should not be confused with intermediate trade, where an export is not made directly to the final consumer, but imported into a third country then reexported with no or little value-added to the final import market.

8. Consider the experience of Gulf Oil Corporation in Korea. Between 1962 and 1980, Gulf was a part owner of Korea Oil Corporation. Much of its profit, however, came from marketing and transportation rather than refining. In 1977, for example, Korea Oil Corporation lost 3.2 billion wons in its refining operation, but Gulf's subsidiary company in trading and transportation more than made up for its share of the loss through earnings from transportation.

9. A trading company which pursues strategy G, without continuing on to strategy H, will become a specialized trading company.

10. This can be examined by the experience curve theory. As a company increases its market share, higher volume allows the company to reduce the relative production cost, thus leading to higher gross margin and increased profits.

Appendix A:
Diversification Indexes

The following are some diversification indexes by product, area, and function used by scholars in their research. The indexes differ from one another in their focus and may well complement the indexes used in this book.

Product Diversification Index

Product Diversification Index 2 (PDI2)

For each firm, Utton[1] defined PDI2 as:

$$PDI2 = 2 \sum_{i=1}^{n} (i \cdot Pi) - 1$$

where Pi = proportion of total sales generated in the ith industry, in rank order such that $Pi \geqslant P_{i+1}$. PDI2 is derived by arranging the industries in order of their relative importance, ranking the segment with highest sales as 1 ($i = 1$) and the lowest as n ($i = n$), and then weighting the proportion of total sales in each industry by its predetermined rank.

Product Diversification Index 3 (PDI3)

PDI3 is also known as the Herfindahl index, and is defined as:

$$PDI3 = 1 / \sum_{i=1}^{n} (Pi^2).$$

Again Pi is the proportion of total sales generated in the ith industry. PDI3 differs from PDI2 in that the proportions are squared. As a result, PDI3 is less sensitive to lower Pi's.

Product Diversification Index 4 (PDI4)

For each firm, I have defined PDI4 in my previous study[2] on the GTC as:

$$PDI4 = 1 - \sum_{i=1}^{n} (Pi^2).$$

PDI4 is formulated so that its value is limited to between 0 and 1 ($0 < PDI4 < 1$).

Area Diversification Index

Area Diversification Index 2 (ADI2)

ADI2 = the number of countries in which the firm is active.

ADI2 is the most basic indicator of geographic diversification, showing simply the number of countries in which the firm has established an active physical presence.

Area Diversification Index 3 (ADI3)

For each firm, ADI3 is defined as:

$$ADI3 = 1/\sum_{j=1}^{n} (Aj^2).$$

ADI3 is designed to measure the concentration of business activities in the seven continents. Aj is the proportion of total branches in each continent. ADI3 is analogous to PDI3, the Herfindahl index.

Area Diversification Index 4 (ADI4)

For each firm, ADI4 is defined as:

$$ADI4 = 1 - \sum_{j=1}^{n} (Aj^2).$$

ADI4 is analogous to PDI4 and can be calculated using the same data as ADI and ADI3.

Functional Diversification Index

Functional Diversification Index 2 (FDI2)

FDI2 is analogous to PDI2, and is defined as:

$$\text{FDI2} = 2 \sum_{i=1}^{n} (i \cdot Fi) - 1$$

where

> n = the number of functional activities conducted by the firm, and
>
> Fi = proportion of total revenues generated by the ith functional activity, in rank order such that $Fi > F_{i+1}$.

Utton's index of diversification is sensitive to the number of functions or activities represented in total revenues.

Notes

1. Utton, Michael A., *Diversification and Competition* (London: Cambridge University Press, 1979).

2. Cho, Dong-Sung, and Hong, Sung-Tae, "The Effects of the Government's Policy on Korean General Trading Companies' Performance: A Quantitative Analysis," *The Korean Business Journal* (Seoul National University) (June 1981).

Appendix B: Export Trading Company Act of 1982

TITLE I—GENERAL PROVISIONS

SHORT TITLE

SEC. 101. This title may be cited as the "Export Trading Company Act of 1982".

FINDINGS; DECLARATION OF PURPOSE

SEC. 102. (a) The Congress finds that—

(1) United States exports are responsible for creating and maintaining one out of every nine manufacturing jobs in the United States and for generating one out of every seven dollars of total United States goods produced;

(2) the rapidly growing service-related industries are vital to the well-being of the United States economy inasmuch as they create jobs for seven out of every ten Americans, provide 65 per centum of the Nation's gross national product, and offer the greatest potential for significantly increased industrial trade involving finished products;

(3) trade deficits contribute to the decline of the dollar on international currency markets and have an inflationary impact on the United States economy;

(4) tens of thousands of small- and medium-sized United States businesses produce exportable goods or services but do not engage in exporting;

(5) although the United States is the world's leading agricultural exporting nation, many farm products are not marketed as widely and effectively abroad as they could be through export trading companies;

(6) export trade services in the United States are fragmented into a multitude of separate functions, and companies attempting to offer export trade services lack financial leverage to reach a significant number of potential United States exporters;

(7) the United States needs well-developed export trade intermediaries which can achieve economies of scale and acquire expertise enabling them to export goods and services profitably, at low per unit cost to producers;

(8) the development of export trading companies in the United States has been hampered by business attitudes and by Government regulations;

(9) those activities of State and local government authorities which initiate, facilitate, or expand exports of goods and services can be an important source for expansion of total United States exports, as well as for experimentation in the development of innovative export programs keyed to local, State, and regional economic needs;

(10) if United States trading companies are to be successful in promoting United States exports and in competing with foreign trading companies, they should be able to draw on the resources, expertise, and knowledge of the United States banking system, both in the United States and abroad; and

(11) the Department of Commerce is responsible for the development and promotion of United States exports, and especially for facilitating the export of finished products by United States manufacturers.

(b) It is the purpose of this Act to increase United States exports of products and services by encouraging more efficient provision of export trade services to United States producers and suppliers, in particular by establishing an office within the Department of Commerce to promote the formation of export trade associations and export trading companies, by permitting bank holding companies, bankers' banks, and Edge Act corporations and agreement corporations that are subsidiaries of bank holding companies to invest in export trading companies, by reducing restrictions on trade financing provided by financial institutions, and by modifying the application of the antitrust laws to certain export trade.

DEFINITIONS

SEC. 103. (a) For purposes of this title—

(1) the term "export trade" means trade or commerce in goods or services produced in the United States which are exported, or in the course of being exported, from the United States to any other country;

(2) the term "services" includes, but is not limited to, accounting, amusement, architectural, automatic data processing, business, communications, construction franchising and licensing, consulting, engineering, financial, insurance, legal, management, repair, tourism, training, and transportation services;

(3) the term "export trade services" includes, but is not limited to, consulting, international market research, advertising, marketing, insurance, product research and design, legal assistance, transportation, including trade documentation and freight forwarding, communication and processing of foreign orders to and for exporters and foreign purchasers, warehousing,

foreign exchange, financing, and taking title to goods, when provided in order to facilitate the export of goods or services produced in the United States;

(4) the term "export trading company" means a person, partnership, association, or similar organization, whether operated for profit or as a nonprofit organization, which does business under the laws of the United States or any State and which is organized and operated principally for purposes of—

(A) exporting goods or services produced in the United States; or

(B) facilitating the exportation of goods or services produced in the United States by unaffiliated persons by providing one or more export trade services;

(5) the term "State" means any of the several States of the United States, the District of Columbia, the Commonwealth of Puerto Rico, the Virgin Islands, American Samoa, Guam, the Commonwealth of the Northern Mariana Islands, and the Trust Territory of the Pacific Islands;

(6) the term "United States" means the several States of the United States, the District of Columbia, the Commonwealth of Puerto Rico, the Virgin Islands, American Samoa, Guam, the Commonwealth of the Northern Mariana Islands, and the Trust Territory of the Pacific Islands; and

(7) the term "antitrust laws" means the antitrust laws as defined in subsection (a) of the first section of the Clayton Act (15 U.S.C. 12(a)), section 5 of the Federal Trade Commission Act (15 U.S.C. 45) to the extent that section 5 applies to unfair methods of competition, and any State antitrust or unfair competition law.

(b) The Secretary of Commerce may by regulation further define any term defined in subsection (a), in order to carry out this title.

OFFICE OF EXPORT TRADE IN DEPARTMENT OF COMMERCE

Sec. 104. The Secretary of Commerce shall establish within the Department of Commerce an office to promote and encourage to the greatest extent feasible the formation of export trade associations and export trading companies. Such office shall provide information and advice to interested persons and shall provide a referral service to facilitate contact between producers of exportable goods and services and firms offering export trade services.

TITLE II—BANK EXPORT SERVICES

SHORT TITLE

Sec. 201. This title may be cited as the "Bank Export Services Act".

SEC. 202. The Congress hereby declares that it is the purpose of this title to provide for meaningful and effective participation by bank holding companies, bankers' banks, and Edge Act corporations, in the financing and development of export trading companies in the United States. In furtherance of such purpose, the Congress intends that, in implementing its authority under section 4(c)(14) of the Bank Holding Company Act of 1956, the Board of Governors of the Federal Reserve System should pursue regulatory policies that—

(1) provide for the establishment of export trading companies with powers sufficiently broad to enable them to compete with similar foreign-owned institutions in the United States and abroad;

(2) afford to United States commerce, industry, and agriculture, especially small- and medium-size firms, a means of exporting at all times;

(3) foster the participation by regional and smaller banks in the development of export trading companies; and

(4) facilitate the formation of joint venture export trading companies between bank holding companies and nonbank firms that provide for the efficient combination of complementary trade and financing services designed to create export trading companies that can handle all of an exporting company's needs.

INVESTMENTS IN EXPORT TRADING COMPANIES

SEC. 203. Section 4(c) of the Bank Holding Company Act of 1956 (12 U.S.C. 1843(c)) is amended—

(1) in paragraph (12)(B), by striking out "or" at the end thereof;

(2) in paragraph (13), by striking out the period at the end thereof and inserting in lieu thereof "; or"; and

(3) by inserting after paragraph (13) the following:

"(14) shares of any company which is an export trading company whose acquisition (including each acquisition of shares) or formation by a bank holding company has not been disapproved by the Board pursuant to this paragraph, except that such investments, whether direct or indirect, in such shares shall not exceed 5 per centum of the bank holding company's consolidated capital and surplus.

"(A)(i) No bank holding company shall invest in an export trading company under this paragraph unless the Board has been given sixty days' prior written notice of such proposed investment and within such period has not issued a notice disapproving the proposed investment or extending for up to another thirty days the period during which such disapproval may be issued.

"(ii) The period for disapproval may be extended for such additional thirty-day period only if the Board determines that a bank holding company proposing to invest in an export trading company has not furnished all the information required to be submitted or that in the Board's judgment any material information submitted is substantially inaccurate.

"(iii) The notice required to be filed by a bank holding company shall contain such relevant information as the Board shall require by regulation or by specific request in connection with any particular notice.

"(iv) The Board may disapprove any proposed investment only if—

"(I) such disapproval is necessary to prevent unsafe or unsound banking practices, undue concentration of resources, decreased or unfair competition, or conflicts of interest;

"(II) the Board finds that such investment would affect the financial or managerial resources of a bank holding company to an extent which is likely to have a materially adverse effect on the safety and soundness of any subsidiary bank of such bank holding company, or

"(III) the bank holding company fails to furnish the information required under clause (iii).

"(v) Within three days after a decision to disapprove an investment, the Board shall notify the bank holding company in writing of the disapproval and shall provide a written statement of the basis for the disapproval.

"(vi) A proposed investment may be made prior to the expiration of the disapproval period if the Board issues written notice of its intent not to disapprove the investment.

"(B)(i) The total amount of extensions of credit by a bank holding company which invests in an export trading company, when combined with all such extensions of credit by all the subsidiaries of such bank holding company, to an export trading company shall not exceed at any one time 10 per centum of the bank holding company's consolidated capital and surplus. For purposes of the preceding sentence, an extension of credit shall not be deemed to include any amount invested by a bank holding company in the shares of an export trading company.

"(ii) No provision of any other Federal law in effect on October 1, 1982, relating specifically to collateral requirements shall apply with respect to any such extension of credit.

"(iii) No bank holding company or subsidiary of such company which invests in an export trading company may extend credit to such export trading company or to customers of such export trading company on terms more favorable than those afforded similar borrowers in similar circumstances, and such extension of credit shall not involve more than the normal risk of repayment or present other unfavorable features.

"(C) For purposes of this paragraph, an export trading company—

"(i) may engage in or hold shares of a company engaged in the business of underwriting, selling, or distributing securities in the United States only to the extent that any bank holding company which invests in such export trading company may do so under applicable Federal and State banking laws and regulations; and "(ii) may not engage in agricultural production activities or in manufacturing, except for such incidental product modification including repackaging, reassembling or extracting byproducts, as is necessary to enable United States goods or services to conform with requirements of a foreign country and to facilitate their sale in foreign countries.

"(D) A bank holding company which invests in an export trading company may be required, by the Board, to terminate its investment or may be made subject to such limitations or conditions as may be imposed by the Board, if the Board determines that the export trading company has taken positions in commodities or commodity contracts, in securities, or in foreign exchange, other than as may be necessary in the course of the export trading company's business operations.

"(E) Notwithstanding any other provision of law, an Edge Act corporation, organized under section 25(a) of the Federal Reserve Act (12 U.S.C. 611-631), which is a subsidiary of a bank holding company, or an agreement corporation, operating subject to section 25 of the Federal Reserve Act (12 U.S.C. 601-604(a)), which is a subsidiary of a bank holding company, may invest directly and indirectly in the aggregate up to 5 per centum of its consolidated capital and surplus (25 per centum in the case of a corporation not engaged in banking) in the voting stock of other evidences of ownership in one or more export trading companies.

"(F) For purposes of this paragraph—

"(i) the term 'export trading company' means a company which does business under the laws of the United States or any State, which is exclusively engaged in activities related to international trade, and which is organized and operated principally for purposes of exporting goods or services produced in the United States or for purposes of facilitating the exportation of goods or services produced in the United States by unaffiliated persons by providing one or more export trade services.

"(ii) the term 'export trade services' includes, but is not limited to, consulting, international market research, advertising, marketing, insurance (other than acting as principal, agent or broker in the sale of insurance on risks resident or located, or activities performed, in the United States, except for insurance covering the transportation of cargo from any point of origin in the United States to a point of final destination outside the United States), product research and design, legal assistance, transportation, including trade documentation and freight forwarding, communication and processing of foreign orders to and for exporters and foreign purchasers, warehousing, foreign exchange, financing, and taking title to goods, when provided in order to facilitate the export of goods or services produced in the United States;

"(iii) the term 'bank holding company' shall include a bank which (I) is organized solely to do business with other banks and their officers, directors, or employees; (II) is owned primarily by the banks with which it does business; and (III) does not do business with the general public. No such other bank, owning stock in a bank described in this clause that invests in an export trading company, shall extend credit to an export trading company in an amount exceeding at any one time 10 per centum of such other bank's capital and surplus; and

"(iv) the term 'extension of credit' shall have the same meaning given such term in the fourth paragraph of section 23A of the Federal Reserve Act."

SEC. 205. On or before two years after the date of the enactment of this Act, the Federal Reserve Board shall report to the Committee of Banking, Housing, and Urban Affairs of the Senate and the Committee on Banking, Finance and Urban Affairs of the House of Representatives the Board's recommendations with respect to the implementation of this section, the Board's recommendations on any changes in United States law to facilitate the financing of United States exports, especially by small, medium-size, and minority business concerns, and the Board's recommendations on the effects of ownership of United States banks by foreign banking organizations affiliated with trading companies doing business in the United States.

GUARANTEES FOR EXPORT ACCOUNTS RECEIVABLE AND INVENTORY

SEC. 206. The Export-Import Bank of the United States is authorized and directed to establish a program to provide guarantees for loans extended by financial institutions or other public or private creditors to export trading companies as defined in section 4(c)(14)(F)(i) of the Bank Holding Company Act of 1956, or to other exporters, when such loans are secured by export accounts receivable or inventories of exportable goods, and when in the judgment of the Board of Directors—

(1) the private credit market is not providing adequate financing to enable otherwise creditworthy export trading companies or exporters to consummate export transactions; and

(2) such guarantees would facilitate expansion of exports which would not otherwise occur.

The Board of Directors shall attempt to insure that a major share of any loan guarantees ultimately serves to promote exports from small, medium-size, and minority businesses or argricultural concerns. Guarantees provided under the authority of this section shall be subject to limitations contained in annual appropriations Acts.

BANKERS' ACCEPTANCES

SEC. 207. The seventh paragraph of section 13 of the Federal Reserve Act (12 U.S.C. 372) is amended to read as follows:

"(7)(A) Any member bank and any Federal or State branch or agency of a foreign bank subject to reserve requirements under section 7 of the International Banking Act of 1978 (hereinafter in this paragraph referred to as 'institutions'), may accept drafts or bills of exchange drawn upon it having not more than six months' sight to run, exclusive of days of grace—

"(i) which grow out of transactions involving the importation or exportation of goods;

"(ii) which grow out of transactions involving the domestic shipment of goods; or

"(iii) which are secured at the time of acceptance by a warehouse receipt or other such document conveying or securing title covering readily marketable staples.

"(B) Except as provided in subparagraph (C), no institution shall accept such bills, or be obligated for a participation share in such bills, in an amount equal at any time in the aggregate to more than 150 per centum of its paid up and unimpaired capital stock and surplus or, in the case of a United States branch or agency of a foreign bank, its dollar equivalent as determined by the Board under subparagraph (H).

"(C) The Board, under such conditions as it may prescribe, may authorize, by regulation or order, any institution to accept such bills, or be obligated for a participation share in such bills, in an amount not exceeding at any time in the aggregate 200 per centum of its paid up and unimpaired capital stock and surplus or, in the case of a United States branch or agency of a foreign bank, its dollar equivalent as determined by the Board under subparagraph (H).

"(D) Notwithstanding subparagraphs (B) and (C), with respect to any institution, the aggregate acceptances, including obligations for a participation share in such acceptances, growing out of domestic transactions shall not exceed 50 per centum of the aggregate of all acceptances, including obligations for a participation share in such acceptances, authorized for such institution under this paragraph.

"(E) No institution shall accept bills, or be obligated for a participation share in such bills, whether in a foreign or domestic transaction, for any one person, partnership, corporation, association or other entity in an amount equal at any time in the aggregate to more than 10 per centum of its paid up and unimpaired capital stock and surplus, or, in the case of a United States branch or agency of a foreign bank, its dollar equivalent as determined by the Board under subparagraph (H), unless the institution is secured either by attached documents or by some other actual security growing out of the same transaction as the acceptance.

"(F) With respect to an institution which issues an acceptance, the limitations contained in this paragraph shall not apply to that portion of an acceptance which is issued by such institution and which is covered by a participation agreement sold to another institution.

"(G) In order to carry out the purposes of this paragraph, the Board may define any of the terms used in this paragraph, and, with respect to institutions which do not have capital or capital stock, the Board shall define an equivalent measure to which the limitations contained in this paragraph shall apply.

"(H) Any limitation or restriction in this paragraph based on paid-up and unimpaired capital stock and surplus of an institution shall be deemed to refer, with respect to the United States branch or agency of a foreign bank, to the dollar equivalent of the paid-up capital stock and surplus of the foreign bank, as determined by the Board, and if the foreign bank has more than one United States branch or agency, the business transacted by all such branches and agencies shall be aggregated in determining compliance with the limitation or restriction".

TITLE III—EXPORT TRADE CERTIFICATES OF REVIEW

EXPORT TRADE PROMOTION DUTIES OF SECRETARY OF COMMERCE

SEC. 301. To promote and encourage export trade, the Secretary may issue certificates of review and advise and assist any person with respect to applying for certificates of review.

APPLICATION FOR ISSUANCE OF CERTIFICATE OF REVIEW

SEC. 302. (a) To apply for a certificate of review, a person shall submit to the Secretary a written application which—

(1) specifies conduct limited to export trade, and

(2) is in a form and contains any information, including information pertaining to the overall market in which the applicant operates, required by rule or regulation promulgated under section 310.

(b)(1) Within ten days after an application submitted under subsection (a) is received by the Secretary, the Secretary shall publish in the Federal Register a notice that announces that an application for a certificate of review has been submitted, identifies each person submitting the application, and describes the conduct of which the application is submitted.

(2) Not later than seven days after an application submitted under subsection (a) is received by the Secretary, the Secretary shall transmit to the Attorney General—

(A) a copy of the application,

(B) any information submitted to the Secretary in connection with the application, and

(C) any other relevant information (as determined by the Secretary) in the possession of the Secretary, including information regarding the market share of the applicant in the line of commerce to which the conduct specified in the application relates.

ISSUANCE OF CERTIFICATE

SEC. 303. (a) A certificate of review shall be issued to any applicant that establishes that its specified export trade, export trade activities, and methods of operation will—

(1) result in neither a substantial lessening of competition or restraint of trade within the United States nor a substantial restraint of the export trade of any competitor of the applicant,

(2) not unreasonably enhance, stabilize, or depress prices within the United States of the goods, wares, merchandise, or services of the class exported by the applicant,

(3) not constitute unfair methods of competition against competitors engaged in the export of goods, wares, merchandise, or services of the class exported by the applicant, and

(4) not include any act that may reasonably be expected to result in the sale for consumption or resale within the United States of the goods, wares, merchandise, or services exported by the applicant.

(b) Within ninety days after the Secretary receives an application for a certificate of review, the Secretary shall determine whether the applicant's export trade, export trade activities, and methods of operation meet the standards of subsection (a). If the Secretary, with the concurrence of the Attorney General, determines that such standards are met, the Secretary shall issue to the applicant a certificate of review. The certificate of review shall specify—

(1) the export trade, export trade activities, and methods of operation to which the certificate applies,

(2) the person to whom the certificate of review is issued, and

(3) any terms and conditions the Secretary or the Attorney General deems necessary to assure compliance with the standards of subsection (a).

(c) If the applicant indicates a special need for prompt disposition, the Secretary and the Attorney General may expedite action on the application, except that no certificate of review may be issued within thirty days of publication of notice in the Federal Register under section 302(b)(1).

(d)(1) If the Secretary denies in whole or in part an application for a certificate, he shall notify the applicant of his determination and the reasons for it.

(2) An applicant may, within thirty days of receipt of notification that the application has been denied in whole or in part, request the Secretary to reconsider the determination. The Secretary, with the concurrence of the Attorney General, shall notify the applicant of the determination upon reconsideration within thirty days of receipt of the request.

(e) If the Secretary denies an application for the issuance of a certificate of review and thereafter receives from the applicant a request for the return of documents submitted by the applicant in connection with the application for the certificate, the Secretary and the Attorney General shall return to the applicant, not later than thirty days after receipt of the request, the documents and all copies of the documents available to the Secretary and the Attorney General, except to the extent that the information contained in a document has been made available to the public.

(f) A certificate shall be void ab initio with respect to any export trade, export trade activities, or methods of operation for which a certificate was procured by fraud.

REPORTING REQUIREMENT; AMENDMENT OF CERTIFICATE;
REVOCATION OF CERTIFICATE

SEC. 304. (a)(1) Any applicant who receives a certificate of review—

(A) shall promptly report to the Secretary any change relevant to the matters specified in the certificate, and

(B) may submit to the Secretary an application to amend the certificate to reflect the effect of the change on the conduct specified in the certificate.

(2) An application for an amendment to a certificate of review shall be treated as an application for the issuance of a certificate. The effective date of an amendment shall be the date on which the application for the amendment is submitted to the Secretary.

(b)(1) If the Secretary or the Attorney General has reason to believe that the export trade, export trade activities, or methods of operation of a person holding a certificate of review no longer comply with the standards of section 303(a), the Secretary shall request such information from such person as the Secretary or the Attorney General deems necessary to resolve the matter of compliance. Failure to comply with such request shall be grounds for revocation of the certificate under paragraph (2).

(2) If the Secretary or the Attorney General determines that the export trade, export trade activities, or methods of operation of a person holding a certificate no longer comply with the standards of section 303(a), or that such person has failed to comply with a request made under paragraph (1), the Secretary shall give written notice of the determination to such person. The notice shall include a statement of the circumstances underlying, and the reasons in support of, the determination. In the 60-day period beginning 30 days after the notice is given, the Secretary shall revoke the certificate or modify it as the Secretary or the Attorney General deems necessary to cause the certificate to apply only to the export trade, export trade activities, or methods of operation which are in compliance with the standards of section 303(a).

(3) For purposes of carrying out this subsection, the Attorney General, and the Assistant Attorney General in charge of the antitrust division of the Department of Justice, may conduct investigations in the same manner as the Attorney General and the Assistant Attorney General conduct investigations under section 3 of the Antitrust Civil Process Act, except that no civil investigative demand may be issued to a person to whom a certificate of review is issued if such person is the target of such investigation.

JUDICIAL REVIEW; ADMISSIBILITY

SEC. 305. (a) If the Secretary grants or denies, in whole or in part, an application for a certificate of review or for an amendment to a certificate, or revokes or modifies a certificate pursuant to section 304(b), any person aggrieved by such determination may, within 30 days of the determination, bring an action in any appropriate district court of the United States to set aside the determination on the ground that such determination is erroneous.

(b) Except as provided in subsection (a), no action by the Secretary or the Attorney General pursuant to this title shall be subject to judicial review.

(c) If the Secretary denies, in whole or in part, an application for a certificate of review or for an amendment to a certificate, or revokes or amends a certificate, neither the negative determination nor the statement of reasons therefor shall be admissible in evidence, in any administrative or judicial proceeding, in support of any claim under the antitrust laws.

PROTECTION CONFERRED BY CERTIFICATE OF REVIEW

SEC. 306. (a) Except as provided in subsection (b), no criminal or civil action may be brought under the antitrust laws against a person to whom a certificate of review is issued which is based on conduct which is specified in, and complies with the terms of, a certificate issued under section 303 which certificate was in effect when the conduct occurred.

(b)(1) Any person who has been injured as a result of conduct engaged in under a certificate of review may bring a civil action for injunctive relief, actual damages, the loss of interest on actual damages, and the cost of suit (including a reasonable attorney's fee) for the failure to comply with the standards of section 303(a). Any action commenced under this title shall proceed as if it were an action commenced under section 4 or section 16 of the Clayton Act, except that the standards of section 303(a) of this title and the remedies provided in this paragraph shall be the exclusive standards and remedies applicable to such action.

(2) Any action brought under paragraph (1) shall be filed within two years of the date the plaintiff has notice of the failure to comply with the standards of section 303(a) but in any event within four years after the cause of action accrues.

(3) In any action brought under paragraph (1), there shall be a presumption that conduct which is specified in and complies with a certificate of review does comply with the standards of section 303(a).

(4) In any action brought under paragraph (1), if the court finds that the conduct does comply with the standards of section 303(a), the court shall award to the person against whom the claim is brought the cost of suit attributable to defending against the claim (including a reasonable attorney's fee).

(5) The Attorney General may file suit pursuant to section 15 of the Clayton Act (15 U.S.C. 25) to enjoin conduct threatening clear and irreparable harm to the national interest.

GUIDELINES

SEC. 307. (a) To promote greater certainty regarding the application of the antitrust laws to export trade, the Secretary, with the concurrence of the Attorney General, may issue guidelines—

(1) describing specific types of conduct with respect to which the Secretary, with the concurrence of the Attorney General, has made or would make, determinations under sections 303 and 304, and

(2) summarizing the factual and legal bases in support of the determinations.

(b) Section 553 of title 5, United States Code, shall not apply to the issuance of guidelines under subsection (a).

ANNUAL REPORTS

SEC. 308. Every person to whom a certificate of review is issued shall submit to the Secretary an annual report, in such form and at such time as the Secretary may require, that updates where necessary the information required by section 302(a).

DISCLOSURE OF INFORMATION

SEC. 309. (a) Information submitted by any person in connection with the issuance, amendment, or revocation of a certificate of review shall be exempt from disclosure under section 552 of title 5, United States Code.

(b)(1) Except as provided in paragraph (2), no officer or employee of the United States shall disclose commercial or financial information submitted in connection with the issuance, amendment, or revocation of a certificate of review if the information is privileged or confidential and if disclosure of the information would cause harm to the person who submitted the information.

(2) Paragraph (1) shall not apply with respect to information disclosed—

(A) upon a request made by the Congress or any committee of the Congress,

(B) in a judicial or administrative proceeding, subject to appropriate protective orders,

(C) with the consent of the person who submitted the information,

(D) in the course of making a determination with respect to the issuance, amendment, or revocation of a certificate of review, if the Secretary deems disclosure of the information to be necessary in connection with making the determination,

(E) in accordance with any requirement imposed by a statute of the United States, or

(F) in accordance with any rule or regulation promulgated under section 310 permitting the disclosure of the information to an agency of the United States or of a State on the condition that the agency will disclose the information only under the circumstances specified in subparagraphs (A) through (E).

RULES AND REGULATIONS

SEC. 310. The Secretary, with the concurrence of the Attorney General, shall promulgate such rules and regulations as are necessary to carry out the purpose of this Act.

DEFINITIONS

SEC. 311. As used in this title—

(1) the term "export trade" means trade or commerce in goods, wares, merchandise, or services exported, or in the course of being exported, from the United States or any territory thereof to any foreign nation,

(2) the term "service" means intangible economic output, including, but not limited to—

(A) business, repair, and amusement services,

(B) management, legal, engineering, architectural, and other professional services, and

(C) financial, insurance, transportation, informational and any other data-based services, and communication services,

(3) the term "export trade activities" means activities or agreements in the course of export trade,

(4) the term "methods of operation" means any method by which a person conducts or proposes to conduct export trade,

(5) the term "person" means an individual who is a resident of the United States; a partnership that is created under and exists pursuant to the

laws of any State or of the United States; a State or local government entity; a corporation, whether organized as a profit or nonprofit corporation, whether under and exists pursuant to the laws of any State or of the United States; or any association or combination, by contract or other arrangement, between or among such persons,

(6) the term "antitrust laws" means the antitrust laws, as such term is defined in the first section of the Clayton Act (15 U.S.C. 12), and section 5 of the Federal Trade Commission Act (15 U.S.C. 45) (to the extent that section 5 prohibits unfair methods of competition), and any State antitrust or unfair competition law,

(7) the term "Secretary" means the Secretary of Commerce or his designee, and

(8) the term "Attorney General" means the Attorney General of the United States or his designee.

EFFECTIVE DATES

SEC. 312. (a) Except as provided in subsection (b), this title shall take effect on the date of the enactment of this Act.

(b) Section 302 and section 303 shall take effect 90 days after the effective date of the rules and regulations first promulgated under section 310.

TITLE IV—FOREIGN TRADE ANTITRUST IMPROVEMENTS

SHORT TITLE

SEC. 401. This title may be cited as the "Foreign Trade Antitrust Improvements Act of 1982".

AMENDMENT TO SHERMAN ACT

SEC. 402. The Sherman Act (15 U.S.C. 1 et seq.) is amended by inserting after section 6 the following new section:

"SEC. 7. This Act shall not apply to conduct involving trade or commerce (other than import trade or import commerce) with foreign nations unless—

"(1) such conduct has a direct, substantial, and reasonably foreseeable effect—

"(A) on trade or commerce which is not trade or commerce with foreign nations, or on import trade or import commerce with foreign nations; or

"(B) on export trade or export commerce with foreign nations, of a person engaged in such trade or commerce in the United States; and

"(2) such effect gives rise to a claim under the provisions of this Act, other than this section.

If this Act applies to such conduct only because of the operation of paragraph (1)(B), then this Act shall apply to such conduct only for injury to export business in the United States".

AMENDMENT TO FEDERAL TRADE COMMISSION ACT

SEC. 403. Section 5(a) of the Federal Trade Commission Act (15 U.S.C. 45(a)) is amended by adding at the end thereof the following new paragraph:

"(3) This subsection shall not apply to unfair methods of competition involving commerce with foreign nations (other than import commerce) unless—

"(A) such methods of competition have a direct, substantial, and reasonably foreseeable effect—

"(i) on commerce which is not commerce with foreign nations, or on import commerce with foreign nations; or

"(ii) on export commerce with foreign nations, of a person engaged in such commerce in the United States; and

"(B) such effect gives rise to a claim under the provisions of this subsection, other than this paragraph.

If this subsection applies to such methods of competition only because of the operation of subparagraph (A)(ii), this subsection shall apply to such conduct only for injury to export business in the United States".

Approved October 8, 1982.

Appendix C:
List of U.S. Export
Trading Companies

State	Name	City	Number
Alabama (5)	Atlas Export Management Corp.	Birmingham	1
	Basin International Inc.	Birmingham	2
	Federal-Mogul World Trade	Jacksonville	3
	International Commodities Corp.	Decatur	4
	Overseas Corp.	Birmingham	5
Arizona (3)	C.M.C.	Phoenix	6
	Mexam Inc.	Tucson	7
	Somos Trading Co.	Phoenix	8
California (46)	Afro-Tech	San Jose	9
	Alexander C. Radcliff & Co.	Monterey	10
	American Global Enterprises, Ltd.	La Canada	11
	Amtrade International Corp.	Cypress	12
	California Distributors International	Santa Ave.	13
	Carlo International	Torrance	14
	Casteel International	Brea	15
	Centrum Commercial Co. Inc.	Los Angeles	16
	Crown-Pacific International	Irvine	17
	EC International	Walnut	18
	Golden Crown Corp.	Beverly Hills	19
	HHS Enterprises Branch of Viron Corp.	Alhambra	20
	HHS Enterprises Etc.	Alhambra	21
	HMC (Hawaiian Motor Company Inc.)	Long Beach	22
	International Export Trading Co., Inc.	Beverly Hills	23
	International Management Advisors	San Pedro	24
	International Software Export Corp.	Sherman Oaks	25
	Jam International	Duarte	26
	Jasko Marketing International Inc.	Mountain View	27
	Latin American Management Co.	San Diego	28
	Latin American Management, Inc.	San Diego	29
	Lindemuth-Brown Trading Co.	San Francisco	30
	Marietta G. Kopplin-Ent	Pasadena	31
	MEDDEX	Los Angeles	32
	Monarch International	San Mateo	33
	Praxis Enterprises	El Toro	34
	Saddleback International Services	Anaheim	35
	San Benito Orchards/Vineyards	Hollister	36
	Security Pacific Trading Corp.	Los Angeles	37

State	Name	City	Number
	Seocal, Inc.	Palo Alto	38
	T.A. Shinn & Associates	Anaheim	39
	The Damar Group	Los Angeles	40
	The Damar Group Agmar International	Los Angeles	41
	The Damar Group Asiapac Exports Division	Los Angeles	42
	The Electric Furnace Co.	Salem	43
	The Export Consultants	West Hollywood	44
	The Heller Group	Beverly Hills	45
	The Trading Industrial Equipment Supply	Huntington Beach	46
	Trade Links International	Los Angeles	47
	U.S. International Marketing Co., Inc.	Bellflower	48
	Unico International Corp.	Garden Grove	49
	Union Fish Co.	San Francisco	50
	United Export Trading Co., Inc.	Los Angeles	51
	Western World Trade, Inc.	Newport Beach	52
	Wolfstein International, Inc.	Los Angeles	53
	117 Inc.	San Francisco	54
Colorado (1)	ICOBA	Denver	55
Connecticut (2)	Elof Hansson Inc.	Norwalk	56
	Intex International Trading Co.	Old Greenwich	57
District of Columbia (7)	Comex Corp.	Washington, D.C.	58
	E. Lipscomb & Associates	Washington, D.C.	59
	Frisco Trading Co.	Washington, D.C.	60
	J.A. Kangwana Co.	Washington, D.C.	61
	Lynx International	Washington, D.C.	62
	Mega Corp.	Washington, D.C.	63
	United States Trading Co.	Washington, D.C.	64
Delaware (2)	Technion International Inc.	Wilmington	65
	Technion International Inc.	Wilmington	66
Florida (23)	Alfonsl Airways & Export, Inc.	Hollywood	67
	Aqua Systems	Tampa	68
	Biscayne Import & Export Co.	Fort Lauderdale	69
	Educational Systems Engineering Corp.	Hialeah	70
	El Bon Enterprise	West Palm Beach	71
	EMEC International, Inc.	Miami	72
	Export Management Associates, Inc.	Panama City	73
	Export Marketing Consultants Inc.	Indialantic	74
	Extraco, Inc.	Miami Lakes	75
	Glasgow Export Sales Inc.	West Palm Beach	76
	Inter-American Autobar Systems, Inc.	Miami	77
	International Technological Services	Boca Roton	78
	Jet Research, Inc.	Pensacola	79
	Jet Research, Inc.	Pensacola	80
	Jet Research, Inc.	Pensacola	81
	Orior Trading Corp.	South Miami	82
	Ricketts Bag Corp.	Tampa	83
	S.B. & P. International Sales Corp.	Lake Park	84

State	Name	City	Number
	Tactician Services Groupe Inc.	Palmetto	85
	Tampa Bay World Trade Co.	Clearwater	86
	Tate & Lyle Enterprises, Inc.	Coral Gables	87
	Welcome Enterprises Corp.	Miami	88
	West Florida West Trading & Consulting	Tampa	89
Georgia (19)	Africanà Export Trading Co.	Atlanta	90
	American International Trading	Augusta	91
	Atlantic Wood International Sales Co.	Savannah	92
	Buchanan Enterprises, Inc.	Atlanta	93
	Chihade International Inc.	Decatur	94
	Dill and Phillips	Atlanta	95
	Exito Trading Co.	Gainesville	96
	Focus Marketing, Inc.	Lawrenceville	97
	Gamma International, Inc.	Atlanta	98
	Gatins International	Atlanta	99
	Goren International, Inc.	Mableton	100
	International Trading Co.	Dalton	101
	Lee International, Inc.	Atlanta	102
	Midworld International Corp.	Tucker	103
	Purvis Lumber Co.	Lenox	104
	Roga International	Rome	105
	Sunbelt Commodities	Harlem	106
	United Chemical & Dairy Exporters Inc.	Decatur	107
	United Egg Producers	Decatur	108
Iowa (3)	Mid States International Corp.	Marion	109
	The American Export Trading Co.	Des Moines	110
	Trademasters Inc.	Twin Falls	111
Illinois (26)	A. Torres Export, Inc.	Chicago	112
	Barens Medical Supplies	Oak Brook	113
	Brost Supply Co.	Chicago	114
	Carberry/Peterson Trading Co.	Chicago	115
	Central Seaway Co., Inc.	Northfield	116
	Comtek, Inc.	Prospect Heights	117
	Denning Electronics Corp.	Hinsdale	118
	First Computer Corp.	Westmont	119
	GBC World Trade	Northbrook	120
	Hasty & Associates	St. Joseph	121
	IHAMCO	Villa Park	122
	Mariner Enterprises, Ltd.	Libertyville	123
	MKI Industries, Inc.	Elk Grove	124
	Paper & Pulp Fiber, Inc.	Desplaines	125
	Rang International Trading Co.	Bensenville	126
	Reliance Auto Supply Co., Inc.	Chicago	127
	Sears World Trade Inc.	Chicago	128
	Seeley Associates Inc.	Chicago	129
	Standard Metal Products	Franklin Park	130
	The Export Department, Inc.	Schaumburg	131
	Trade Development Corp. of Chicago	Chicago	132
	Unimex Co.	Willowbrook	133
	United Executives International	Desplaines	134
	United Pacific Corp.	West Chicago	135
	Unironex Corp.	Elk Grove Village	136
	Worldwide Exports	Hinsdale	137

State	Name	City	Number
Kansas (1)	Data Communications Export Co.	Mission	138
Kentucky (1)	The Summit Co.	Louisville	139
Maryland (1)	Interface Associates, Inc.	Arnold	143
Massachu-setts (3)	Andrew-Douglas Corp.	Sharon	140
	B & G Associates	Holyoke	141
	Bariston Inc.	Salem	142
Michigan (25)	American Manufacture Export Co.	Grand Rapids	144
	Amtrex Corp.	Ann Arbor	145
	Berge International Group	Bloomfield Hills	146
	Chrysler Corp. Interparts	Detroit	147
	Degnore & Associates, Inc.	West Bloomfield	148
	DEXIMA	Belleville	149
	Drucker Associates Inc.	Grosse Pointe Woods	150
	DSA of America Inc.	Southfield	151
	E.D.M. Importing/Exporting Group	Lansing	152
	Engelhard Corp.	Southfield	153
	Exportise Ltd.	Swartz Creek	154
	Gamls Corp.	Davisburg	155
	Independent Utility Systems/Michigan	Mt. Pleasant	156
	International Marketing Group	Muskegon	157
	International Multifoods Corp.	Minneapolis	158
	International Trade Exchange Corp.	Detroit	159
	John Ford & Associates, Inc.	St. Clair Shores	160
	Kmart Trading Services	Troy	161
	METALPO	Troy	162
	Midwest Export Trading Co.	Grosse Pointe Park	163
	Noram International	Sault Ste. Marie	164
	R. Robb International Assoc., Inc.	Southfield	165
	Transverse, Inc.	Grand Rapids	166
	U.S. Export Sales Corp.	Clawson	167
	Usbitds Inc.	Temperance	168
Minnesota (9)	AMEX Inc.	Minneapolis	169
	Cesco Export Inc.	Minneapolis	170
	Control Data Commerce International	Minneapolis	171
	F & E Enterprises Inc.	Bloomington	172
	H & H Exports, Inc.	Duluth	173
	Marketing Specialists International Ink	Minneapolis	174
	Phillippi Equipment Co.	Golden Valley	175
	Seven Seas Trading Co.	St. Paul	176
	Simer International, Inc.	Minneapolis	177
Missouri (5)	Bartlett Trading Corp.	Kansas	178
	Dynacon, Inc.	St. Louis	179
	Gateway International Export Co.	St. Louis	180
	Onyx International	St. Louis	181
	Universal Trading Group, Ltd.	St. Louis	182

State	Name	City	Number
North Carolina (17)	A.B. Andrews	Research Triangle Park	183
	Aeroglide Americas, Inc.	Cary	184
	Carolina Galvanizing Corp.	Aberdeen	185
	Casalee America Corp.	Winston-Salem	186
	Casalee Trading Corp.		187
	Dunn Enterprise Winston Salem, Inc.		188
	Gulfstream Export Co.	Sanford	189
	Laurdan Group International	High Point	190
	Leggette Associates, Inc.	Rocky Mount	191
	North Carolina International Traders	Graham	192
	Pam Trading Corp.	Kernersville	193
	Rabya-USA, Inc.	Durham	194
	Sequence (USA) Co. Ltd.	Durham	195
	Sieco (Southern Import-Export Co.)	Greensboro	196
	Smi Corp.	Burlington	197
	Southeastern International I/E Corp.	Lumberton	198
	Southern Import/Southco International	Wilmington	199
Nebraska (3)	International Trading Co. Inc.	Fremont	200
	International Trading Co. Inc.	Fremont	201
	Valmont Industries Inc.	Valley	202
New Jersey (24)	Absecam International, Inc.	Atlantic City	203
	Continental Export Trading Corp.	Red Bank	204
	Demirkaya International	Kingston	205
	Devero Co. of America	Cherry Hill	206
	E.C. Tradeco	Camden	207
	Engelhard Industries Division	Iselin	208
	Expomar International Inc.	East Brunswick	209
	Hydra-Tech Pumps, Inc.	Mt. Holly	210
	ICS Contractors Supply, Inc.	Summit	211
	Marketerc, Inc.	Hoboken	212
	Med-X International Inc.	Cresskill	213
	Millmaster-Onyx International, Inc.	Fairfield	214
	MMI, Inc.	Manasquan	215
	Nevco (a division of U.S. Industries)	Garfield	216
	Overseas Sales Service	Lakewood	217
	Pioneer Co., Inc.	Tenafly	218
	Plantation Holdings Corp.	Kinnelon	219
	Rathore Corp.	Randolph	220
	Regal Products Inc.	Willingbord	221
	Talteck, Inc.	Vincentown	222
	The Greegg Company, Ltd.	Hackensack	223
	Trans American Trading Firm Inc.	Jersey City	224
	Ultramar Marketing Corp.	Tennent	225
	Webtech Inc.	Robbinsville	226
New York (43)	A & S International Marketing Co.	Brentwood	227
	American Steel Export Co., Inc.	New York	228
	Arpol Petroleum Co.	New York	229
	Ashiley Polymers International Inc.	New York	230
	Betadyne International	New York	231
	Brewster Leeds & Co.	New York	232
	Bush Plastics Division	Salamania	233
	Carbomin Group, Inc.	New York	234

State	Name	City	Number
	Chew International Group	New York	235
	Export Agencies International Corp.	Freeport	236
	Export/Import International	New Paltz	237
	Fitzpatrick & Weller Inc.	Ellicottville	238
	Gate Group USA/IKE Savitt Assoc.	New York	239
	Jonas Aircraft and Arms Co. Inc.	New York	240
	Ketchum & Co. International	New York	241
	✓Ketchum & Co. International, Inc.	New York	242
	Kingson International Co. Inc.	Harrison	243
	Larsen International, Inc.	Rochester	244
	Lobel Chemical Corp.	New York	245
	Marc J. Fisher Inc.; Duke International Trade	New York	246
	Meridien Marketing Corp.	New York	247
	Merona Corp.	New York	248
	Miltan Export Corp.	New York	249
	Nigma Corp.	Syracuse	250
	Opera Trading Corp.	New York	251
	P.R. Angel, Inc.	New York	252
	Pace International Inc.	Mineola	253
	Port Authority Trading Co.	New York	254
	Power Automotive Industries Inc.	Farmingdale	255
	R & H Schaefer Industries, Inc.	Great Neck	256
	R.A. Rodriguez Inc.	Garden City	257
	S.A. Libra, Inc.	Buffalo	258
	Seraphim, Saleem and Khella, Inc.	New York	259
	Sillcox International Corp.	New York	260
	Syracuse Export Import Co.	Devitt	261
	T.T. Lee Assoc.	New York	262
	Tanbank International	New York	263
	The Bankertowne Co., Inc.	West Hempstead	264
	Uni-World Industries inc.	New York	265
	✓Uni-World Industries Inc., One World	New York	266
	Unit Sales Co.	Pomona	267
	Weft Industries	New York	269
	World Auto Parts, Inc.	Buffalo	270
Ohio (21)	Allied International	Lorain	271
	Banner World Trading Co.	Cleveland	272
	Buded International, Inc.	Cincinnati	273
	C.A.M.E.—Consortium of Appliance	Cleveland	274
	Crest Aluminum Products Inc.	Eastlake	275
	Dealers Dairy Product Co.	Cleveland	276
	Export America Inc.	Canton	277
	Intermarket Corp.	Cleveland	278
	International Projects, Inc.	Toledo	279
	L & E International	Toledo	280
	L.J. Minor Corp.	Cleveland	281
	Mark International, Inc.	Cleveland	282
	N.B. Carson & Co., Inc.	Cleveland	283
	Nagel Trading Co.	Akron	284
	Owens-Illinois	Toledo	285
	Paper Corp. of U.S.	Cincinnati	286
	The Trexler Rubber Co.	Ravenna	287
	Transport Systems, Inc.	Cincinnati	288

State	Name	City	Number
	World Trade Services, Inc.	Cleveland Heights	289
	Yen Enterprises Inc.	Cleveland	290
	Zwm International Trade Co.	Westlake	291
Oklahoma (1)	Service Engineering International	Oklahoma	292
Pennsylvania (7)	Barter Systems International	Youngwood	293
	Custom Wrought Products Co.	Greentown	294
	Du Wayne Melrotes	Butler	295
	Manleatracon, Inc.	Pittsburgh	296
	Orion	Pittsburgh	297
	Sprague & Henwood International	Scranton	298
	Trade Marketing International Ltd.	Pittsburgh	299
South Carolina (14)	Business Resources International Co.	Georgetown	300
	C.W. Dunaway & Co.	Columbia	301
	Charleston Steel & Metal Trading Co.	Charleston	302
	Crescent International, Inc.	North Charleston	303
	Export Trading Associates	Seneca	304
	H & L Enterprises	Charleston	305
	Hibri Enterprises, Inc.	Hanahan	306
	I.T.M.	Columbia	307
	Insulations International, Inc.	Lake Wylie	308
	Southeast Overseas Trade Group	Greenville	309
	Stevenson-Hopkins International Trade	Columbia	310
	Trans World Investments, Ltd.	West Columbia	311
	Tru-Tech International, Inc.	Spartanburg	312
	Wimsco Inc.	Columbia	313
Tennessee (6)	Abdullah Diversified Marketing Inc.	Victor Abdullah	314
	Export Trading Corp.	Moscow	315
	Impex International Andrew Johnson	Howard Russell	316
	Interex	Nashville	317
	Kagiya Trading Co. Ltd. of America	Nashville	318
	Trans-Global Trading Corp.	Knoxville	319
Texas (10)	DHB Enterprises Inc.	Houston	320
	I-T-U Trading, Inc.	Houston	321
	International Development Inc.	Stafford	322
	International Trade & Business Relations	Austin	323
	Marint—Marketing International	Plano	324
	Nelley International	Houston	325
	Ramya Enterprises	Houston	326
	Shah International	Houston	327
	Supply Export International Corp.	Houston	328
	Texas First Intercontinental Trading	Dallas	329
Virginia (12)	American Products International, Inc.	McLean	330
	Combyte Inc.	Alexandria	331
	CVA Inc. of Springfield	Springfield	332
	ECI International, Ltd.	Herndon	333
	Equipment USA, Inc.	Herndon	334
	Hemisphere International Trading Co.	Alexandria	335
	International Affairs, Inc.	McLean	336

State	Name	City	Number
	Jenkins Export/Import	Fairfax	337
	Oasis International Inc.	Vienna	338
	Precision Export Trading Co.	Richmond	339
	Trade Development International Inc.	Alexandria	340
	World Trade Associates, Inc.	Arlington	341
Wisconsin	DMT World Trade, Inc.	Waukesha	342
(6)	Dummann World Trade Co. Inc.	Milwaukee	343
	George Zaferos, Inc.	Brown Dear	344
	National Fluid Power Association	Milwaukee	345
	PAD Ltd.	Milwaukee	346
	Techtran International, Inc.	Appleton	347
West Virginia	Auric Enerco Co.	Morgantown	348
(2)	Harold L. Porter & Assoc. International	Ceredo	349

Source: *Export Trading Companies, Contact Facilitation Service Directory* (Washington, D.C.: International Trade Administration, U.S. Department of Commerce, June 1984).

DATA ANALYSIS

1. general analysis

2. type for each hypothesis to be supported

IV. ACTION—MAILING LISTS

	Check System	Change	Delete	Add
	[ ]	[ ]	[ ]	[ ]

Initial _____ _____ _____ _____

Other Action Taken _____ Date _____ Initial _____

GML _____

Name Mr. Ms. Dr. _____

Title _____

Firm/Department _____

Address _____

_____

(CITY)   (STATE)   (ZIP)

Mailing Lists _____

Interests Lists _____

Glossary

chonghap-mooyeok-sangsa   In Korea, the term *general trading company* is generally used to describe the companies designated as *chonghap-mooyeok-sangsa,* the official Korean name. We will use the term *general trading company* in this book to describe the Korean companies.

European trading company   See *European trading house.*

European trading house   The history of most European traders can be traced to the export merchant. Therefore, the term *European trading house* is used extensively to describe them throughout the book. This term, however, is used interchangeably with *European trading company* when contemporary activities are described.

export management company   Term used to describe a trade intermediary in the United States. It is usually small, privately held, thus undercapitalized, and product- or area-specific. More important, most EMCs neither take title to the goods they export nor provide a "one-stop" exporting service, although that is not the case among the larger ones.

export merchant   Old, established term to describe a trader, usually serving as an agent for the manufacturer, who plays the role of principal in transactions with foreign customers. In the 1800s, European export merchants took over most of the responsibilities of the manufacturers by providing a wide range of services in trading, and the term *export merchant* was gradually replaced with *trading house.* As a result of this evolution, the trading house now offers multiple services related to trading, such as providing the manufacturer with cash to cover the cost of the goods, giving credit: to the customer on its own account, and taking on the financial risks by assuming the title of the transactions.

export trading company   The term officially used by the U.S. government in its Export Trading Company Act of 1982. This term is strictly used to describe the U.S. trading companies based on the act.

foreign trade corporate company   Term used by the Turkish government in instituting its version of the GTC.

general trading company   This term is used in two ways in this book. First, it is used to describe a trading firm that regards itself, or is regarded by others, as a general trading company whatever its definition might be. For example, the Korean general trading companies, Taiwanese large trading companies, Thai international trading companies, and U.S. export trading companies are regarded as general trading companies, their equivalent, or their modification. This book acknowledges that various trading companies are called general trading companies and uses the term accordingly. Second, this book develops a conceptual definition of the general trading company; this definition will be found in chapter 2.

international trading company   Officially used by the Thai government to describe the large trading companies in Thailand designated by the government for promoting export activities.

large trading company   A direct translation of the term for Taiwanese trading companies designated by their government for export promotion and takeover of import activities from foreign importers.

sogo-shosha   Widely accepted as a term to describe the nine or so largest trading companies in Japan.

trader   See *trading firm.*

trading company   This term has been used in two ways in the export world. In the broad sense, it applies to a firm that buys goods in one national market to resell at a profit in foreign markets. In this context, trading company has an identical meaning with trading house, although the latter has the historical connotation of the European export merchant while the former does not. In a more specialized sense, the term has traditionally been used to describe a handful of Japanese trading firms that have extensive marketing networks all over the world.[1] Since one of the objectives of this book is to develop the concept of the trading company, rather than to describe the nature of specific trading companies, we will use the term *trading company* with a broad meaning.

trading firm   Describes a company that buys goods in one national market to resell at a profit in foreign markets. Sometimes called a *trader.* This is the broadest among the similar terms, encompassing all categories of trading organizations. In this book, manufacturing firms that also engage in exportation are considered trading firms.

trading house   See *trading company* and *export merchant.*

Note

1. Colin McMillan and Sydney Paulden, *Export Agent,* 2nd ed. (Hampshire, England: Gower Press, 1974), p. 27.

Bibliography

English Titles

Abbot, Alden, "Missing the Boat on Export Trading Companies," *Regulation* (Nov./Dec. 1982), 39-44.

Abegglen, James C., *Management and Worker: The Japanese Solution* (Toyko: Kodansha International, 1973).

Alexandries, C.G., and Moschis, George P., *Export Marketing Management* (New York: Praeger Publishers, 1977).

Anansiriprapha, Kheeseng, "General Trading Companies and Manufactured Exports from Thailand," Master's thesis, Thammasat University, Bangkok, 1983.

Ansoff, H. Igor, *Corporate Strategy: Business Policy for Growth and Expansion* (New York: McGraw-Hill, 1965).

Balassa, Bela, "Trade Liberalization and Revealed Comparative Advantage," Manchester, The Manchester School of Economic and Social Studies, May 1965.

Bangkok Post, November 17, 1978, and September 14, 1982.

Becker, Tom, & Porter, James L., "Selling, ETC," *Sales & Marketing Management* (July 4, 1983), 44-48.

Bello, Daniel C., and Williamson, Nicholas C., "The American Export Trading Company: Designing A New International Marketing Institution," *Journal of Marketing* (Fall 1985), 60-69.

Biggadike, Ralph, "The Risky Business of Diversification," *Harvard Business Review* (July 1980).

Buckley, Peter J., and Casson, Mark, *The Future of the Multinational Enterprise* (London: The Macmillan Press Ltd., 1976).

Business Asia, "Taiwan's Trading Firms Offer Competition and New Sales Routes," November 17, 1978; "Taiwan's Big Companies Still No Match for Japanese Giants," September 24, 1982.

Business Week, "Here Come the New Yankee Traders," (May 30, 1983), 22.

Cashflow, "ETC Growth Should Bolster U.S. Exports" (July/August 1984), 9.

Cateora, Philip R., and Hess, John M., *International Marketing*, 3rd ed. (Homewood, Ill.: Richard D. Irwin Inc., 1975).

Caves, Richard, and Uekusa, Masu, *Industrial Organization in Japan* (Washington, D.C.: The Brookings Institution, 1976).

Chandler, Alfred D., Jr., *Strategy and Structure: Chapters in the History of the American Industrial Enterprise* (Cambridge, Mass.: M.I.T. Press, 1962).

———. *The Visible Hand: The Managerial Revolution in American Business* (Cambridge, Mass.: Harvard University Press, 1977).

Channon, Derek F., and Jollard, M., *Multinational Strategic Planning* (New York: Amacon, 1979).

Chase, Marilyn, "U.S. Company Hopes to Profit Japanese-Style," *Wall Street Journal (International)* (February 18, 1981), 18.

Chemical Week, "Export Trading Companies" (June 27, 1984), 92-94.

Chew, Ralph H., "Export Trading Companies: Current Legislation, Regulation and Commercial Bank Involvement," *Columbia Journal of World Business* (Winter 1981), 42-47.

Cho, Dong-sung, *"International Facility Planning: Regarding the Application of Scientific Approaches,"* Harvard Business School, 1977.

———. "Evaluation of the Korean Government Strategies to Develop General Trading Companies," Conference Proceedings of the Asia-Pacific Conference of the Academy of International Business, December 1979.

———. "Stages of Internationalization: The Case of Korean Enterprise," *Korean Journal of International Business* (July 1980).

———. "The Anatomy of the Korean General Trading Company," *Journal of Business Research* (July 1984).

———. "Diversification Strategies of the GTC and the MNC," Working Paper 9-785-005, Division of Research, Harvard Business School, July 1984.

———. "Incentives and Restraint: Changing Government Roles in Bilateral Direct Investment between Korea and the United States," in Karl Maskorwitz, ed., *From Patron to Partner: The U.S.-Korean Economic and Business Relationship* (Lexington, Mass.: Lexington Books, 1984).

———. "The Sogo-shosha Transplanted," *Euro-Asia Business Review*, July 1985.

Cifelli, Anna, "A Fallback Plan for Aiding U.S. Exporters," *Fortune* (April 2, 1984), 66.

Clark, Rodney, *The Japanese Company* (New Haven: Yale University Press, 1979).

Council for Economic Planning and Development, *Taiwan Statistical Data Book 1980* (Taipei, 1981).

Dizzard, John W., "Sears' Humbled Trading Empire," *Fortune* (June 25, 1984), 71-75.

Dymza, William A., *Multinational Business Strategy* (New York: McGraw-Hill Book Company, 1972).

Farmer, R.N., and Richman, B.M., *Comparative Management and Economic Progress* (Homewood, Ill.: Richard D. Irwin, Inc., 1965).

Fayerweather, John, *International Marketing* (Englewood Cliffs, N.J.: Prentice-Hall, 1970).

Fieldhouse, D.K., *Unilever Overseas* (Stanford, Calif.: Hoover Institution Press, 1978).

Fortune, "The 50 Leading U.S. Exporters" (August 6, 1984), 37.

Franko, L, G., *The European Multinationals* (London: Harper and Row Ltd., 1976).

General Electric Annual Report, 1983.

Glaman, Kristofer, *Dutch-Asiatic Trade, 1620–1740* (Copenhagen: Danish Science Press, 1958).

Gort, M., *Diversification and Integration in American Industry* (Princeton University Press, 1962).

Heenan, David A., and Perlmutter, Howard V., *Multinational Organization Development* (Reading, Mass.: Addison-Wesley Publishing Company, 1979).

Holten, Richard H., "The Role of Competition and Monopoly in Distribution: The Experience in the United States," in Lee E. Preston, ed., *Social Issues in Marketing* (Glenview, Ill.: Scott, Foresman and Company, 1968).

Hood, N., and Young, S., *The Economics of Multinational Enterprise* (London: Longman Group Ltd., 1979).

Industry Week, "Sears Trades on a Name" (March 19, 1984), 83.

International Banker, "The Export Trading Company Act" (February 17, 1983), 11-46.

International Management, "Here Come the U.S. Trading Firms" (January 1984), 16-18; "A Costly Startup for Sears World Trade" (September 1984), 8.

Johnson, Chalmers, *MITI and the Japanese Miracles* (Stanford, Calif.: Stanford University Press, 1982).

Jung, Ku-Hyun, "The Sogo Shosha: Can it be Exported (Imported)?" Discussion series, Yonsei University, April 1982.

Kanji, Haitani, *The Japanese Economic System* (Lexington, Mass.: D.C. Heath and Company, 1976).

Kaplan, Eugene J., *Japan—The Government-Business Relationship* U.S. Department of Commerce, Washington, D.C., 1972.

Keegan, W.J., *Multinational Marketing Management* (Englewood Cliffs, N.J.: Prentice-Hall, 1980).

————. "Strategic Marketing: International Diversification versus National Concentration," *Columbia Journal of World Business* (Winter 1977), 119-130.

Kolde, Endel J., *International Business Enterprise* (Englewood Cliffs, N.J.: Prentice-Hall, 1973).

Kotler, Philip, *Marketing Management* (Englewood Cliffs, N.J.: Prentice-Hall, 1980).

Lachica, Eduardo, "Unlikely American Exporter: Japan," *Wall Street Journal (International)* (November 11, 1981), 10.

Lagesse, David, "Bank Board Escrow Rule Stirs NY Ire," *American Banker* (December 12, 1983), 1, 47.

Love, J., ed., *Jane's Major Companies of Europe*, (London: Jane's Yearbook, 1975).

Maher, Philip, "GE Starts Trading Company Venture," *Industrial Marketing* (May 1982), 24.

Maher, Philip, "Trading Companies: A U.S. Export Panacea?" *International Marketing* (October 1982), 59-68.

Majaro, Simon, *International Marketing* (London: George Allen & Unwin Ltd., 1977).

Marubeni Corporation, *The Unique World of the Sogo-shosha*, Tokyo, 1978.

————. *Marubeni Monthly* (Tokyo) (January 1980—March 1981).

Mill, James, *The History of British India* (London: James Madden, 1958).

Mukherjee, Ramkrishna, *The Rise and Fall of the East India Company, A Sociological Approach* (Berlin: VEB Deutscher Verlag der Wissenschaften, 1958).

Norton, Robert E., "Sears Unit Looking to Trade for the World," *American Banker* (December 12, 1983), 1-2, 6, 14.

Ozawa, T., *Multinationalism: Japanese Style* (Princeton, N.J.: Princeton University Press, 1979).

Pascale, Richard T., and Athos, Anthony G., *The Art of Japanese Management: Applications for American Executives* (New York: Simon and Schuster, 1981).

Pawluk, M.A., "How One Company Manages Its Countertrade," Remarks to International Symposium on Development in International Trade and Export Incentives, Istanbul, Turkey, January 16, 1985.

Porter, Michael, *Competitive Strategy* (New York: the Free Press, 1980).

Reischauer, Edwin, *Japan, the Story of a Nation*, revised ed., (New York: Alfred A. Knopf, 1974).

Roehl, Thomas, "The General Trading Companies: A Survey of Japanese Language Sources," Paper presented at the Lake Wilderness Workshop on the Japanese Economy, Seattle, Washington, July 14, 1980.

Rossman, Marlene L., "Exporting Trade Company Legislation: U.S. Response to Japanese Foreign Market Penetration," *Journal of Small Business Management* (October 1984), 62-66.

Rothermund, Dietmar, *Asian Trade and European Expansion in the Age of Mercantilism* (New Delhi: Manohar Publishers, 1980).

Rumelt, Richard, "Strategy, Structure and Economic Performance," Division of Research, Harvard University, Graduate School of Business Administration, 1974.

Salter, Malcolm, and Weinhold, Wolf, *Diversification through Acquisition* (New York: The Free Press, 1979).

Schooler, Robert D., "The Determinants of Foreign Opportunity Attractiveness," *International Management Review* (University of Missouri, April-May 1974).

Simon, Herbert, *Administrative Behavior*, 2nd ed., (New York: MacMillan Company, 1961).

Steck, Robert N., "Export Trading Companies," *D & B Reports* (May/June 1984), 42-43.

Stobaugh, Robert B., "Where in the World Should We Put that Plant," *Harvard Business Review* (January-February 1969).

————. "How to Analyze Foreign Investment Climates," *Harvard Business Review* (November-December 1969).

Stopford, J.M., and Wells, L.T., Jr., *Managing the Multinational Enterprise* (New York: Basic Books, Inc., 1972).

Terpstra, Vern, *International Marketing* (Hinsdale, Ill.: Dryden Press, 1978).

Tokyo Economic Information Service Co., Ltd, *Sogo-shosha Yearbook 1976* (Tokyo, 1976).

Tsurumi, Yoshi, *Sogo-shosha: Engines of Export-based Growth* (Montreal: The Institute for Research on Public Policy, 1980).

U.S. Department of Commerce, *The Multinational Corporation* Vol. I and II, U.S. Department of Commerce Publication, Washington, D.C., 1972.

Utton, M.A., *Diversification and Competition* (London: Cambridge University Press, 1979).

Vernon, Raymond, *Sovereignty at Bay* (New York: Basic Book, Inc., 1971).

Vogel, Ezra F., *Japan as Number One* (Cambridge, Mass.: Harvard University Press, 1979).

Weber, John A., "Worldwide Strategies for Market Segmentation," *Columbia Journal of World Business* (Winter, 1974), 107-116.

Wiechman, U.E., *Marketing Management in Multinational Firms* (New York: Praeger Publishers, 1976).

Williamson, Oliver, *Markets and Hierarchies: Analysis and Antitrust Implications* (New York: The Free Press, 1975).

Yoshihara, Kunio, *Sogo-shosha: the Vanguard of the Japanese Economy* (Tokyo: Oxford University Press, 1982).

Yoshino, Michael Y., *Japan's Multinational Enterprises* (Cambridge, Mass.: Harvard University Press, 1976).

Young, Alexander K., *The Sogo-shosha: Japan's Multinational Trading Companies* (Boulder, Colo.: Westview Press, Inc., 1979).

————. "Internationalization of the Japanese General Trading Companies," *Columbia Journal of World Business* (March 1974).

Japanese Titles

Aida, Hideo, *Sogo-shosha* (General Trading Company) (Tokyo: Nihon Keizai Shimbunsha, 1977).

Fujii, Mitsuo, Nado, *Keieishi-Nippon* (Japanese Business History) (Tokyo: Nihon Hyoronsha, 1972).

Iwata, Ryushi, *Nihon Teki Keiei No Hensei Genri* (The Principles of Japanese Management (Tokyo: Bunchin Do, 1978).

Kinugasa, Yoho, *Nihon Kigyo No Kokusaika Senryaku* (The Internationalization Strategy of Japanese Companies (Tokyo: Nihon Keizai Shimbunsha, 1979).

Kubo, Gen, *Sogo-shosha To Sekaizatatsu Gun* (Sogo-shosha and the World's Conglomerates), (Tokyo: Tokyo Nunoi Shuppan Kabushiki Gaisha, 1975).

Kunito, Yoshimasa, *Sumitomo Shonin* (Tradesman of Sumitomo) (Tokyo: Kobunsha, 1966).

Muramatsu, Shijo, *Kigyo Gobenron* (Theory of Business Mergers) (Tokyo: Dobunkan Shuppan Kabushiki Gaisha, 1973).

Nikkei Business, ed., *Shosha: Huyu no Zidai* (Trading Companies; Age of Winter) Tokyo: Nihon Keizai Shimbunsha, 1983).

Nikko Research Center, *Mitsubishi Shoji No Kenkyu* (Study on Mitsubishi Trading Company) (Tokyo: Toyo Keizai Shimposha, 1980).

Seikei, Tsushinsha, *Sogo-shosha Nenkan, 1974* (Annual Statistics of Sogo-shosha, 1974) (Tokyo: Seikei Tsushinsha, 1974).

Sekai Keizai Joho Service, *Sekai Shuyo Kigyo No Kaigai Katsudo To Kankyo* (The Overseas Activities and Environment of the World's Major Enterprises) (Tokyo: Kekai Keizai Service, 1973).

Shosha Kino Kenkyukai Hen, *Gendai Sogo-shosha Ron* (Theory of Modern Sogo-shosha) (Tokyo: Toyo Keizai Shimposha, 1976).

————. *Shin Sogo-shosha* (New Sogo-shosha) (Tokyo: Toyo Keizai Shimposha, 1981).

Sogo-shosha Kaigai Toshi Chosa Kenkyukai, *Kaigai Jigyo Katsudo To Sogo-shosha* (Overseas Business Activities and Sogo-shosha) (Tokyo: Kikai Shinko Kyokai Keizai Kenkyujo, 1975).

Takada, Tsutomu, *Gendai No Sogo-shosha* (Today's Sogo-shosha) (Tokyo: Nihon Jitsugyo Shuppansha, 1975).

Toba, Kinichiro, Yaku, *America Keieishi Jo, Ge* (Business History of America, Parts 1, 2), (Tokyo: Toyo Keizai Shimposha, 1977).

Tsuda, Shincho, *Nihon Teki Keiei No Ronri* (The Logic of Japanese Management) (Tokyo: Chuo Keizaisha, 1978).

Tsugai, Yoshimasa, *Mitsui Bussan Kaisha No Keieishi Teki Kenkyu* (Study on the Business History of Mitsui Trading Company) (Tokyo: Toyo Keizai Shimposha, 1974).

Yasuoka, Shigeaki, *Nihon No Zaibatsu* (Japan's Conglomerates) (Tokyo: Nihon Keizai Shimbunsha, 1976).

Yonekawa, Shinichi, *Keiei Shigaku* (Business History) (Tokyo: Toyo Keizai Shimposha, 1973).

———. *Europe, America, Nihon No Keizai Hudo* (Business Climate of Europe, America, and Japan) (Tokyo: Yuhikaku, 1978).

Korean Titles

Baek, Kwon-Ho, "Kukjehwa Kiup'ui Dakakuha Bigyo" (Comparison of Diversification among International Firms) Master's thesis, Seoul National University, 1983.

Ban, Byung-Kil, *Dakukjek Kieplon* (Theory of Multinational Enterprise) (Seoul: Pakyongsa, 1973).

———. *Kukje Marketing Lon* (International Marketing) (Seoul: Pakyongsa, 1980).

Cho, Dong-Sung, "Jungbu'ui Chonghap Sangsa Yuksung Banghyang'ie Sangsa Kyungyung Sunggua'ei Michin Yunghyang'ei Daehan Gueryangjiuk Bunsuk" (Quantitative Analysis of the Effect of Government Policy on GTC Performance) *Kyungyung Nonjip* (The Korean Business Journal), (Seoul National University, June 1981).

———. "Hanguk Chonghap Muyuk Sangsa'ui Kyungyung'ei Daehan Sulmun Chosa" (A Questionnaire on Korean GTC's Management Situation), *Kyungyung Sarei Yungu* (The Practice of Management) (Seoul National University, June 1981).

———. "Hanguk Chonghap Muyuk Sangsa'ui Haewei Jisa Kuanli" (The Management of Overseas Branches of Korean GTC), *Kyungyung Sarei Yungu* (The Practice of Management) (Seoul National University, December 1982).

———. "Chonghap Muyuk Sangsa'ui Jeongbo Kwanli" (On the Management of Information by General Trading Company), *Trade Promotion Policy in the 1980s*, (Seoul: Korea International Economic Institute, July 1982).

———. Kyungyoung Jeongchaek-kwa Changki Jeonryak Kyehoek (Business Policy and Long-range Strategic Planning) (Seoul: Youngji Moohwasa, 1983).

———. *Hankook-eui Chonghap Muyuk Sangsa: Bonjil-kwa Jeonryak* (Korea's General Trading Company: Concept and Strategy) (Seoul: Bupmoonsa, 1983).

———. *Hankook-eui Chonghap Muyuk Sangsa: Jedo-wa Kwanli* (Korea's General Trading Company: System and Management) (Seoul: Bupmoonsa, 1983).

Daehan Muyuk Jinhung Gongsa, *Kyungjengkuk Suchul Marketing Junlyak* (Export Marketing Strategy of Competitive Countries) (Seoul: Daehan Muyuk Jinhung Gongsa, 1977).

Han, Hui-Young, *Marketing Guanlilon* (Marketing Mangement) (Seoul: Dasan Chulpansa, 1980).

Hanguk Euihuan Eunheng, *Ilbon Jonghap Sangsa'ui Guinung'gua Jojik* (The Function and Organization of Japanese Sogo-shosha) (Seoul: Hanguk Euihuan Eunheng, 1979).

Hanguk Muyuk Hyuphei, *Muyuk Yungam 1978, 79, 80, 81, 82* (Annual Trade Statistics 1978, 79, 80, 81, 82) (Seoul: Hanguk Muyuk Hyuphei, 1978, 1979, 1980, 1981, 1982).

Hanguk Sanup Unheng, *Jonghap Sangsa'ui Hyunhuang'gua Guinung Ganghwa Bangan* (The Reality of the General Trading Company and Recommendation for Strengthening its Functions) (Seoul: Hanguk Sanup Unheng, 1978).

Hong, Sung-Tae, "Kiup'ui Kyungyung Dakaghwa'ei Gan'han Yungu" (A Study on Business Diversification), Master's thesis, Seoul National University, 1981.

Jung, Ku-Hyun, "Ouri Nara Suchul Marketing'ui Hyunhwang'gua Ganghwa Bangan" (The Reality of Korea's Export Marketing and Recommendation for its Strengthening), *Kyungyunghak Yungu* (Korean Management Review) (Seoul: Korean Association of Business Administration, 1982).

Kim, Byung-Sun, "Hanguk Giup'ui Haiwei Jikjup Tuja" (Foreign Direct Investment of Korean Firms), Master's thesis, Seoul National University, 1980.

Kim Won-Su, *Marketing Guanlilon* (Marketing Management (Seoul: Kyungmun sa, 1981).

Kim, Yung-Do, "Dakukjuk Kiup'gua Jonghap Muyuk Sangsa'ui Huangyung Mit Junlyak'ui Bigyo Bunsuk" (Comparative Analysis of the Environment and Strategy Between the Multinational Enterprise and the General Trading Company), Master's thesis, Seoul National University, 1982.

Ko, Shi-Chen, Il Bon'ui Jonghapsangsa (Japan's Sogo-shosha) (Seoul: Kukje Kyungje Yunguwon, 1978).

Kukje Kyungje Yunguwon, *Pal Ship Yundai Plant Suchul Chokjin'oul Wuihan Daiung Junlyak* (Strategy for Promoting Export of Plant in the 80's) (Seoul: Kukje Kyungje Yunguwon, 1979).

Kukje Sangse Chusik Heisa, *Jonghap Sangsa'ui Guinung'gua Shilje* (The Function and Reality of General Trading Company) (Seoul: Kukje Sangsa, 1982).

Lee, Yung-Sun, *Ouri Nara Suchul Sangpum'ui Bigyo Ouwei Bunssek'gua Jenmang* (Analysis and Prospect of Comparative Advantage of Korean Export Products) (Seoul: Kukje Kyungje Yunguwon, 1980).

Oh, Sang-Lak, and Lim, Jong-Won, *Choesin Markeging Guanlilon* (New Marketing Management) (Seoul: Muyok Kyungyungsa, 1975).

Index

About the Author

Dong-Sung Cho, BBA (1971) from Seoul National University and DBA (1976) from Harvard Business School, spent two years at 'Gulf Oil Corporation as a senior planner before joining in 1978 the faculty of Seoul National University, where he is now an associate professor of international business and business policy. He has authored eight books and more than thirty articles, which include *International Resources Management* (1981—chosen as the best book of the year in economics/business) and *International Business* (1984). He has extensively researched and lectured overseas, serving as a senior research fellow at the Institute of Developing Economy of Tokyo in 1983, a visiting associate professor of general management at the Harvard Business School in 1983-84, and a visiting professor at INSEAD, France, in 1985. He has also served as an advisor to the Ministry of Energy and Resources since 1980, and to the Bureau of Transportation Vehicles, the Ministry of Commerce and Industry, since 1984.